PREHISTORIC ROC
OF NORTHUMBE

VOLUME 2

STAN BECKENSALL
BA, DIP.ED, FSA(SCOT)

WITH A FOREWORD BY RICHARD BRADLEY, MA,FSA,MIFA,FSA(SCOT)
PROFESSOR OF ARCHAEOLOGY, UNIVERSITY OF READING

STAN BECKENSALL 4 LEAZES CRESCENT HEXHAM NE46 3JX

1

FOREWORD

The prehistoric rock carvings of northern Britain have been known for well over a century, but they attracted little attention until recently. There have been valuable surveys of the rock art found in several areas of the country, including southern and western Scotland, parts of Yorkshire and Northumberland. A striking feature of nearly all this work is that it has been carried out by part-time archaeologists: energetic enthusiasts who have recorded this evidence to a very high standard.

It is surprising that their work has taken so long to attract the attention of an academic audience, but there are many reasons for this. Archaeologists have been happier at studying settlements and artefacts than working with the natural features of the terrain, and they have written a prehistory with a strong emphasis on monuments but little sense of place. They have been too interested in the archaeology of farmers and all too wary of interpreting the lifestyles of mobile people. They have been afraid that the study of ancient art might impugn their credentials as objective scientists.

The students of British rock carving have not been beset by these inhibitions. As prehistorians gain more confidence, they are starting to realise the true significance of this material. Rock art is perhaps the one medium which can bring together the specialised motifs associated with great monuments like chambered tombs and the simpler designs inscribed on the natural landscape. There is enormous potential for creative research.

Stan Beckensall has been one of the most patient and thorough of all the recorders of British rock art, and his eye for the details of individual carvings is as keen as his grasp of the countryside as a whole. He has discovered many of the rock carvings described in this book and has added many new details to our knowledge of older finds. He has recorded his observations patiently over many years, so that he has now compiled one of the largest and most accessible bodies of information on this important subject. In writing this book, he has made a considerable contribution to our knowledge of prehistoric Britain.

More important, his work conveys the excitement of discovery and his feeling for the carvings and those who made them. This is not the prerogative of those who practice archaeology as a career. He shares his work with a much wider public, and this is what makes this book so attractive. Like the carvings themselves, it is for everyone.

Richard Bradley

VOLUME 2: BEANLEY TO THE TYNE
================================

INTRODUCTION

Motifs that have been known for years as 'cup and ring marks'
in Northumberland and elsewhere have fascinated people, given
rise to speculation about what they mean, been largely
neglected by writers about Prehistory, and are now taking their
rightful place as an art form and 'language' that is unique in
Prehistoric culture.
Art and symbolic expression are always difficult concepts for
us to handle; when we try to get into the minds of people who
lived so long ago, we are cluttered with our own backgrounds
and assumptions. It is very different from studying tools,
weapons, field systems and settlement sites.
The great range of symbol, design and area covered in
Northumberland makes this county central to an understanding of
who made them, and why.
When people began in the 19th. Century to discover cup and ring
marks, most were in the north of the county, but they rightly
predicted that more would be found in the south on the
sandstones. This book shows the extent of new discoveries, and
re-locates earlier ones, showing that the basic symbols of
cups, rings and grooves continue, although some rare designs,
based on rosettes and rectangles do not appear, nor do the very
large, multiple concentric rings.
All are again on sandstone: not a single example has been found
on the igneous rocks of the Cheviots or on whinstone, perhaps
because it was too difficult to peck designs on to them.
The discovery of new sites and re-recording of others has
resulted from the interest of a few individuals, whose powers
of observation and willingness to report their finds have made
this survey possible. No professional group has been involved
in this work. Searches of some areas have been systematic and
thorough, but some discoveries have been accidental. Today's
distribution map will no doubt be added to, as more people
become aware of what to look for.

This volume provides data: the first step to understanding what
the markings mean and why they were put there. What they look
like, their distribution and relationship to other Prehistoric
monuments are the only 'scientifc' factors that can be
recorded. The rest is hypothesis based on these facts, and
that must be tested against all sites in Britain, and beyond.

There are some interesting general observations to be made
about the area covered in this book:
a) Some motifs occur with burials, all early Bronze Age.
Markings on some cist covers and the presence of 'portable'
small marked stones in burial cairns point to a religious use.
The problem here, though, is that past recording is not always
precise, and even the enlarged food vessel full of cremated
bone in the Corby Crags rock-shelter, with a pecked groove on
the floor and a large cup and ring on the rock overhang does

3

not absolutely tie the urn to the symbol, despite the care with which the site was excavated, although the association is highly probable.
b) Cup marks on standing stones, such as Matfen, Goatscrag 'four poster' and Fontburn stone circle, indicate a religious use of the symbol, although there is little chance that any further excavation of such disturbed monuments would reveal much.
c) Many boulders and small portable stones are elaborately marked, but they are out of context. There are so many in Northumberland, some dug up in fields, some built into walls (including a castle wall), some from Iron Age and Roman sites, that one wonders where they were originally. Of special interest are those that are marked on two faces. Elsewhere, such stones in a firmer context are in burial cairns, but there is an argument that claims that all of them could have been made earlier, and re-used either accidentally or deliberately. That cannot be proved, either.
d) Fascinating though these portables are, most symbols are to be found in situ on outcrop rock, and a careful analysis of their geographical position gives us, literally and figuratively, firmer ground to work on.
The choice of high places with good views, and the spread of marked rocks along natural routes, indicates that they are used by people whose lives were at least partly nomadic, and the spread and types of flint implements show that they were hunters as well as food growers.
The trouble is that 'they' cannot be pinned down to specific tribes or centuries: in Prehistory the same areas can be used for hundreds of years, so we don't know when a particular rock had its symbols pecked onto it, or whether the whole range of symbols was made in one go. But what unifies them is that the same motifs recur, from the simple cup to the more elaborate designs that suggest that someone was artistic and innovative. If we use the evidence of flints and pottery in Northumberland, then add excavated burials, the greatest evidence points to Early Bronze Age people rather than Neolithic, but from other parts of Britain we know that some symbols were in use among Neolithic communities.
Someone was marking the routes- to define territorial divisions, hunting grounds, the way to sacred places?
e) An examination of the outcrop sites has shown how many marked rocks must have been lost through quarrying. These quarries are generally small, often circular areas, and in great numbers. The same sandstones also contain coal, and bell pit mining is extensive. Associated with such local industries are hollow ways and other evidence of transportation of stone and coal.
f) Much of the high ground has thin soil, is only of marginal agricultural value, and the survival of monuments may be attributed to this. However, there is evidence of different kinds of rig and furrow ploughing, intended for the growth of arable crops, which has become fossilised by its use as pasture, and some of it has reverted to boggy , sour land.

4

Reeds, bracken, nettles and thistles vie with one another, and modern forestry takes over areas that are not useful for alternative crops. Many rock surfaces must have been covered up or removed, and one must take into account that there were more marked rocks than there are now, and still the possibility that those covered up will reappear. Observable changes in land use mean that it is very difficult to understand what the vegetation cover would have been like at the time the markings were made, although if there were sufficient excavation and pollen analysis on some sites, it would help to clarify this.

g) We are left with the reality of the markings themselves, and these can be examined in detail. The trouble is that they do not tell us of their origin. It is a language of signs, not pictures of real things, and it is possible that the people who made them were not aware of the origin-only their significance. They knew what they **meant**.

For us they can be like an ink-blot test: we read into them something of ourselves. Fair enough, but it isn't objective and can't be proved. An even bigger danger is crack-pot theory, such as a recent one that tries to make them copies of crop circles! Stupidity, arrogance and the search for sensationalism that may help to bring in the cash are not unknown in the interpretation of symbolism.

So it is back to the safety of accurate recording, which this book is about. It will provide more data for the inevitable speculation and hypotheses that will follow. The mystery is unlikely to end, because we don't have enough information, and all our knowledge continues to bring us nearer to our ignorance. But I welcome any sane attempt that uses the data wisely to float new ideas.

The work of recording these sites has been shared with Irene and Ian Hewitt, and I am grateful to Ian for access to his unpublished dissertation on these and other sites in Britain (Bournemouth Polytechnic, 1991).
Further use of this data and other research will arise from a Reading University project directed by Professor Richard Bradley, with whom I am cooperating, in 1992.

ARRANGEMENT OF DATA
===================

For some, the illustrations may be the most interesting part of this book, but as it is a complete record, each site is referenced with a National Data Base number and Grid Reference to enable the rocks to be accurately located. You are recommended to use the Ordnance Survey Pathfinder series of maps with this book.

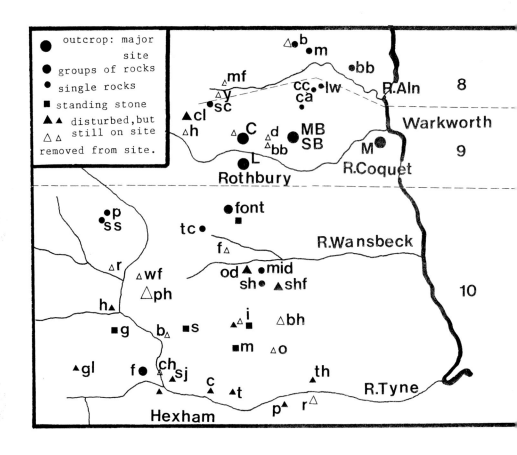

SITES COVERED IN VOLUME 2

There are initial capitals for the major sites: Cartington, Lordenshaw, Millstone Burn, Snook Bank and Morwick, all in Region 9.

Other sites have initial lower-case letters. In Region 8, from west to east: Yetlington, Mountain Farm, Beanley, Midstead, Black Bog Dean.

Region 9: Harbottle Peels, Clennell, Scrainwood, Debdon Whitefield, Black Burn, Caller Crag(ca), Corby Crag(cc), Lemmington Wood and Lamp Hill(together as lw).

Region 10: Padon Hill, Sunday Sight, Tod Crag, Fontburn, Fawns, Reenes, West Farm, Pitland Hills, Old Deanham, Middleton, Shaftoe(sh), Shortflatt(shf), Houxty, Goatstones, Barrasford, Swinburn, Ingoe, Black Heddon(bh), Matfen, Ouston, Greenlee Lough, Frankham, Chesters, Hexham, St. John Lee, Corbridge, Thornborough, Prudhoe, Ryton, Throckley.

Off the map, on the Cumbrian border, is Hartleyburn.

In the regional study that follows, each site is given a National Data Base number, devised by I. and I.M. Hewitt, and a Grid Reference. The full records of each site, including bibliography, are deposited with County Monuments record.

REGION 8: BEANLEY MOOR TO ALNWICK.
===================================
BEANLEY MOOR (Public access)

HOO593. NU 1015 1855. This large dome of sandstone outcrop, lying among many others, about 100m. east of the Ringses hillfort, was reported by Tate in the 1860s and re-located by I.and I.M. Hewitt. There are hut circles, field divisions and small quarries on poor land.
The markings are unimpresssive: some cups difficult to distinguish from natural indentations, and two have rings. The rock, recorded in two parts (E and W), showing the motifs, has a great view of the surrounding country, including Old Bewick Moor and Hepburn.
A very well-designed slab (HOO591) was found in the same area in 1864, covered with vegetation, and taken to Alnwick Castle with every pick mark clear and uneroded. It has always been referred to as a 'cist cover', but no details were given. Another stone (HOO592) with 4 penannulars, again contrasting with the simple motifs on the outcrop, was found at the same time in a field drain, and again linked, without detail, with burial.

WHITTINGHAM

HOO607. NU 0527 1275. MOUNTAIN FARM. A cist capstone from a burial was covered with incised circles, but there are no further details, and the stone is lost.
HOO606. NU 032 107. YETLINGTON LANE. Disturbed and placed at the side of a field, this stone was moved to Humbleton, Wooler.
MIDSTEAD (private land)

HOO641. NU 1243 1546. Named after a now-destroyed house, the outcrop lies on a slope with good views, close to settlement sites with hut circles and low walls.
ALNWICK

HOO629. NU 177 162. BLACK BOG DEAN. (Private). Unusually, this small outcrop lies at the side of a stream, and is now almost totally obscured by planting.

Beanley means the bean field or clearing. Whittingham is Hwita's peoples' homestead, and Alnwick is the farm on the River Aln.

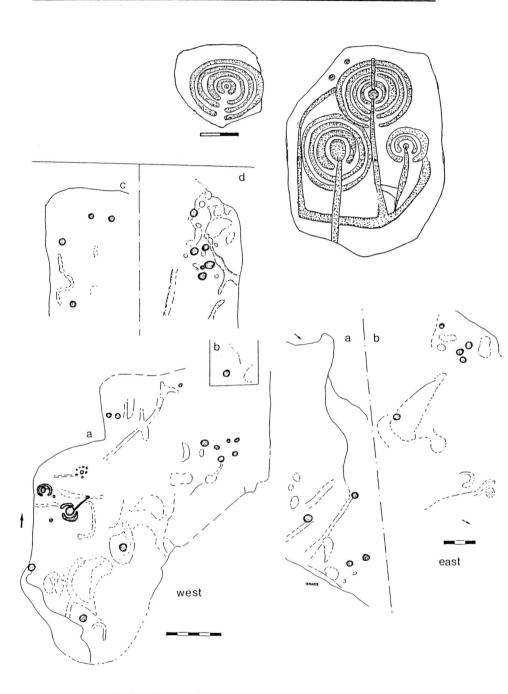

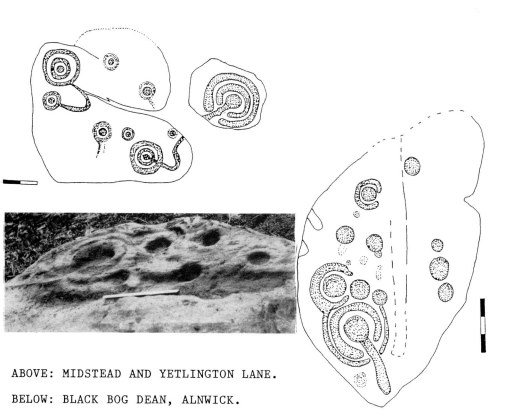

ABOVE: MIDSTEAD AND YETLINGTON LANE.

BELOW: BLACK BOG DEAN, ALNWICK.

Scale: decimetres.

REGION 9
========
FROM HARBOTTLE TO MORWICK
=========================
This great expanse of land generally follows the River Coquet.
The motifs first appear on the edge of the volcanic Cheviot
Hills, follow the sandstone outcrops, and end at the
extraordinary spread of spirals on the cliff face at Morwick
before the Coquet reaches the North Sea.
Beginning with an oval shape pecked on to the inside slab of a
'food vessel' cist at Harbottle Peels, the distribution of the
motifs includes boulders and slabs, which could have been
moved. They keep to places that are on natural routeways and
places from which there are extensive views, they mix with
settlement sites, defensive sites and round burial mounds, can
be traced for miles in some places, and then disappear, finally
reaching the cliffs at a fording place on the Coquet, where the
motifs change bewilderingly to art more reminiscent of Irish
passage graves, but furthest away from the apparent source.
Their survival depends on how much the land on which they are
implanted has been rejected as arable or ignored as a source of
quarrying, but the motifs do make one of the finest stretches
of rock art anywhere in the country.

H00725. NT 943 047. HARBOTTLE PEELS. (Site destroyed).
Because this is one of the ubiquitous Canon Greenwell's sites, the slab that he dug up from a multiple burial site is now at the British Museum. He clearly recorded its position on the south side of a cist, facing inward, describing it as 'reniform' or foot-shaped. There is a similar shape at Old Bewick (site 3a) on outcrop, with other motifs.
The site contained 4 cists and 6 unburnt and 3 burnt bodies, and all pottery was food vessel type.
ALWINTON/NEWTON/CLENNELL COTTAGES (Private) ·
On a ridge, with wide views to the Cheviots and south, these four marked boulders have been disturbed by field clearance, so it is not possible to say in what context they were.
H00721. NT 9379 0689 , taken from a pile of field clearance stones, is now in private hands.
H00722 and 3 NT 9358 0702 are now in a wood, having been cleared from a possible cairn. One stone has only a single cup mark, and is not illustrated here (H00723).
H00724. NT 9365 0720. was found beside the Clennell trackway among field clearance stones. 'Clennell' is a hill clear of weeds or harmful growth.
H00726. NT 9984 0986. SCRAINWOOD, ALNHAM (Access allowed)
On outcrop rock overlooking Scrainwood Farm and a breadth of countryside around, this is an outcrop or earthfast boulder in pasture. 'Scrainwood' means the shrews' or villains' wood.
H00727. NT 9988 0994. SCRAINWOOD QUARRY is the resting place of this portable small slab, but we don't know where it came from. There has been extensive clearance for arable and pasture in this area, as well as some minor quarrying.

The Scrainwood sites are shown on the right hand inset, and the Clennell sites on the left. Refer to the Pathfinder Series.

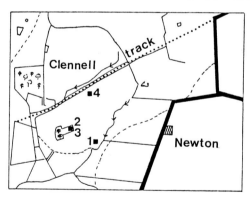

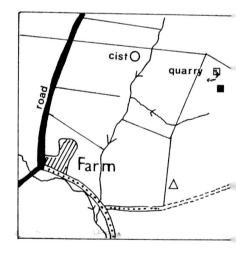

■ Marked rock

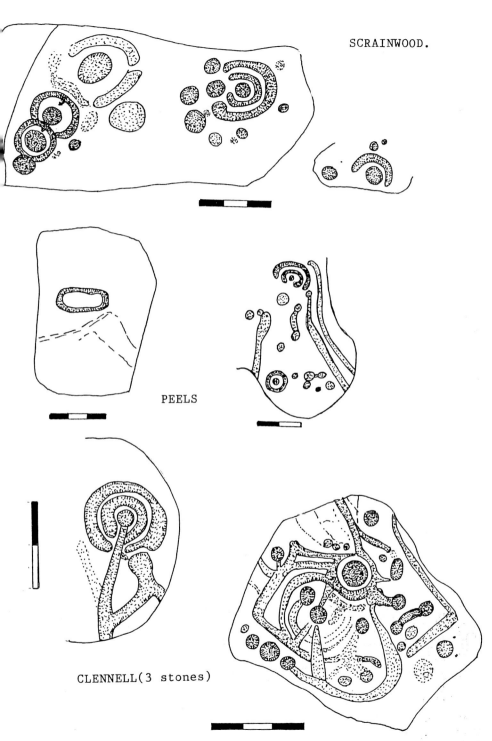

SCRAINWOOD.

PEELS

CLENNELL(3 stones)

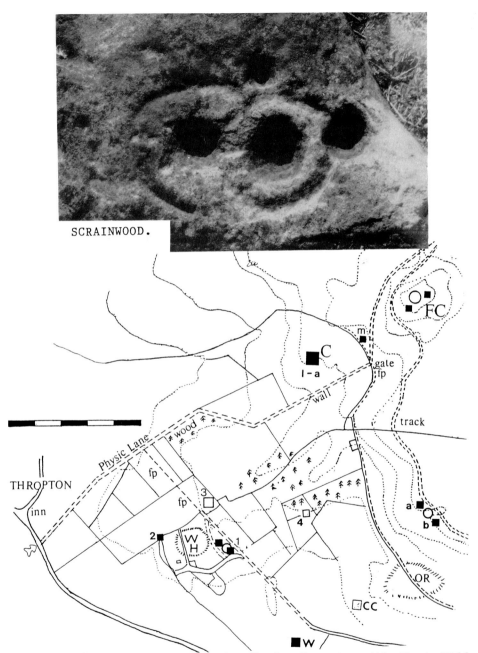

SCRAINWOOD.

The map shows the area north of the Coquet, with West Hills (WH), Chirnells (c), Football Cairn (FC), Westcliffe (W), Cartington Cove (CC), and the Carriageway. OR is Old Rothbury enclosure. Cairns are marked with a circle, sites as a black square, and sites that are now destroyed or grown over are marked with a hollow square.

12

THE ROTHBURY AREA

In the Rothbury area begins one of the most concentrated series of rock motifs in Northumberland. They are not so elaborate or aesthetically pleasing as those in the Wooler area, but their positioning is most interesting.

Because the area around Rothbury is popular and well served with good footpaths, this section includes more detail on how to reach individual marked rocks. Some will be disappointing: a few scattered cup marks are not very exciting, but all discoveries are important, and may represent only a fraction of what was once there.

NORTH OF THE COQUET.

To the north of the River Coquet, which channels itself into a gorge in the east, is the high moorland of Cartington Moor. Parts of this retain Prehistoric sites, including cairns, standing stones, a rock overhang in which flints have been found, a cave with motifs destroyed by quarrying, and hillforts. The moor has easy access by a carriageway built by Lord Armstrong, who was responsible for altering much of the landscape in the building of Cragside and its extensive park. Planted woodland alternates with heather and bare rock, with the lower slopes utilized for farming. Housing has also encroached on the moor, and the sandstone has proved good for quarrying.

H00662. NU 037 053. Cartington.

The most northerly find was near Cartington Castle, where an unusual triangular slab, now at Newcastle Museum of Antiquities, was found face downward in a field, with its peck marks fresh. Medieval rig and furrow, now pasture, has left little else on the surface, but there was a spectacular discovery of a hollowed out coffin burial covered with stone, north of the farm buildings ,east of the Lorbottle road.

Access to the sites where there is still something to see is from many directions, but it will help the walker if you start at Thropton village. Physic Lane, a green road, gives access to the western part. Follow the lane up the hill, and when you have almost reached the wall that divides pasture from heather, look to the left where a thin band of sandstone shows intermittently through grass on a slope, surmounted by gorse. This is Chirnells Moor, (a)-(j), NU 0418 0275 (H00663), where 8 groups of markings were recorded in 1933, and are the most interesting in this area. (The name Childerlund means the children's land). Irene and Ian Hewitt discovered another one beyond the wall to the moor this year (k). This outcrop is reached through the gate at the end of Physic Lane (turn left), and follow the continuation of the ridge NE to the next site:

H00665. NU 0459 0303. Football Cairn, the name given to a sadly dilapidated large burial mound with a massive cist at its centre. 16.2 metres to the east on the slope, careful rubbing has revealed many motifs, including multiple concentric circles. 23m. west of this is a triangular-shaped boulder, 66cm. high, with a large, deep cup, and to the SW are two

outcrops with faint markings, (a) 50m bearing 28 deg. to the cist, and (b) 44m. at 70 deg.

H00672. CARTINGTON CARRIAGEWAY, (a) - (c). (Public)

Previously known as 'Cartington Plantation', the closeness of the rocks to the Carriageway makes the new name more appropriate. The hard track leads from Football Cairn, and at NU 0460 0222, 45m. west of the track there is a plateau of heather with little scattered stone, where just before the land drops sharply away is a cup marked stone, possibly a fallen standing stone. Between this and the next marked rock are 3 cairns, probably barrows, that lie between an earth wall and a path leading downhill to a huge block of stone and a quarry. ESE. of the narrow path, only 12m. from the carriageway is (b), at NU 0470 0418. Although the drawing shows this covered with cups and rings, they only came to light with wax rubbing, but more have been revealed than when the stone was first found. (c) is an isolated mark on outcrop further east.

The views from the ridge are beautiful and extensive, with a particularly good view of Old Rothbury settlement below. The easiest way to find the next sites is to go back to Physic Lane by following the track downhill past this settlement, via Brae Head, or to approach from Hillside Road West.

Off Physic Lane is a signposted footpath on the left at the end of a small wood. Cross two fields with stone stiles to:

NU 0369 0208 Westhills Camp

The 'camp' is an Iron Age enclosure, accessible by footpath.

H00667. NU 0380 0212 Westhills Camp 1 (a)-(e). (Private)

By a stone burial cairn, tree covered, are two cup-marked rocks, (a,b), an uncertain-age rectilinear pattern, (c), and a grooved rock,(d). On outcrop rock between cairn and camp, mostly grown over, are cups and rings,(e).

H00668 NU 0395 0208. Site 2.

In a triangular enclosure is is a poor specimen of faint cup marks on a boulder, SE of a wall bordering pasture.

H00669 NU 0385 0225. Site 3.

On rock outcrop, 200m. NNE from the camp centre, are 3 sets of marks, now covered with vegetation, including 8 cups with vertical sides and an oval.

H00670 NU 0421 0221 Site 4 Bracken Wood.(Private)

There are supposed to be two cups and weathered rings.

H00671. NU 0444 0186 Cartington Cove.

The cave or overhang was destroyed by quarrying, but it was reported to have some unspecified cup and ring markings inside it. This makes it the third such site in Northumberland.

H00664. NU 0553 0293 Addeyheugh.

A large cup- marked boulder lies in a cairnfield as part of an alignment. It lies east of a public footpath from Hillside Road, that crosses the moor in a roughly northerly direction, towards Debdon farm, linking up with the carriageway.

H00666. NU 0423 0173 Westcliffe House.

The house and grounds are private, and permission would have to be sought to view these two outcrops with, mainly, cup marks.

Coquet means cock's wood. Cartington is Certa's people's hill.

A VIEW FROM LORDENSHAW, ON THE SOUTH OF THE RIVER COQUET, TO
CARTINGTON MOOR. ROCK ART USUALLY OVERLOOKS WIDE LANDSCAPES.

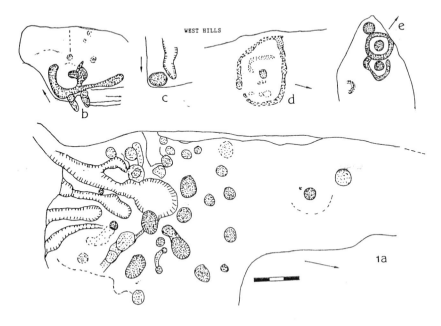

WEST HILLS CAMP, WHERE RATHER POOR EXAMPLES OF ROCK ART SHARE A
SITE WITH A HILLFORT AND BURIAL CAIRN.

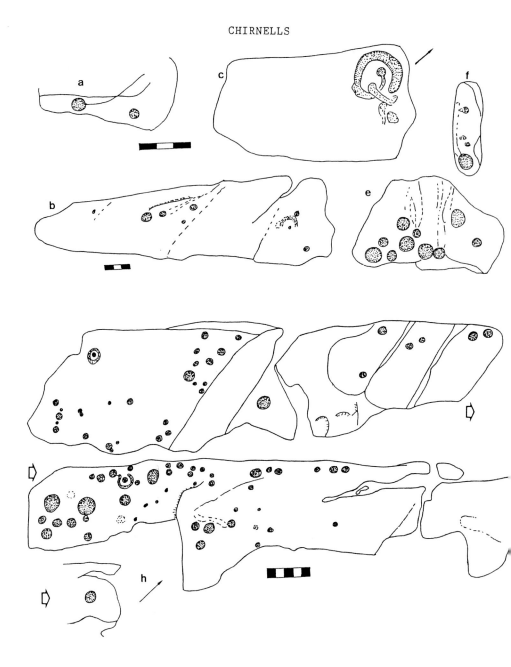

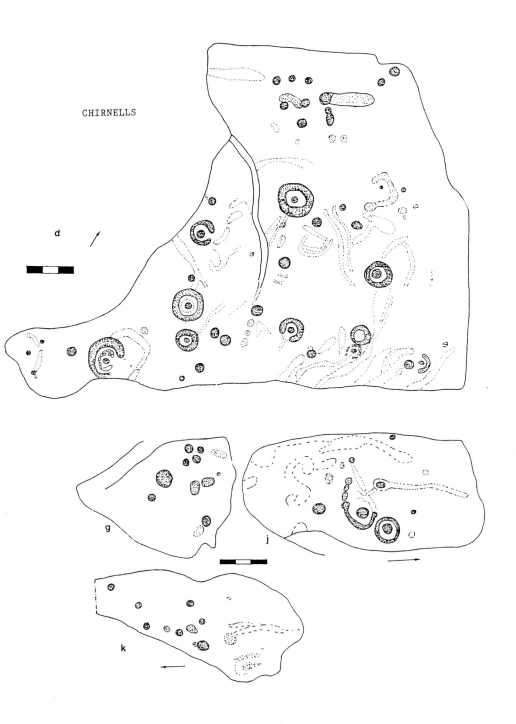

CHIRNELLS

d

g

j

k

CHIRNELLS

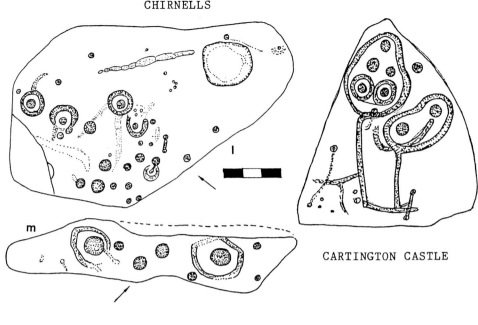

CARTINGTON CASTLE

WESTCLIFFE HOUSE

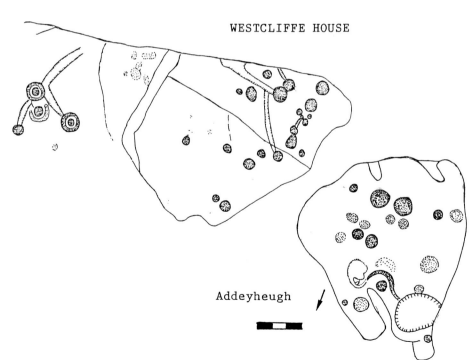

Addeyheugh

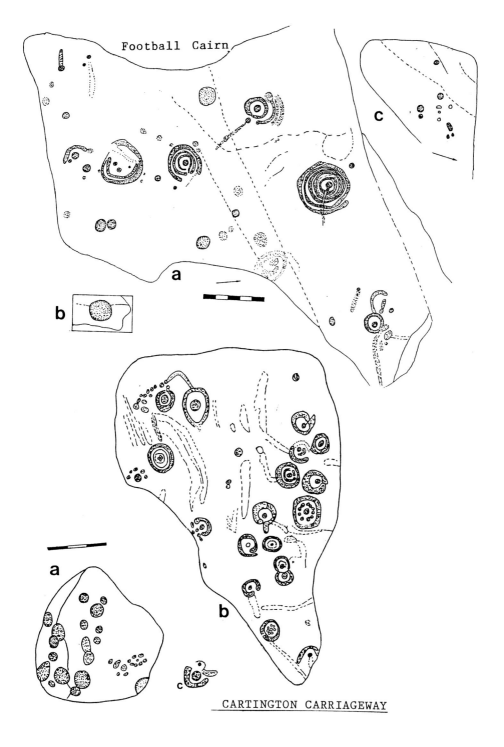

Football Cairn

a

b

c

a

b

c

CARTINGTON CARRIAGEWAY

19

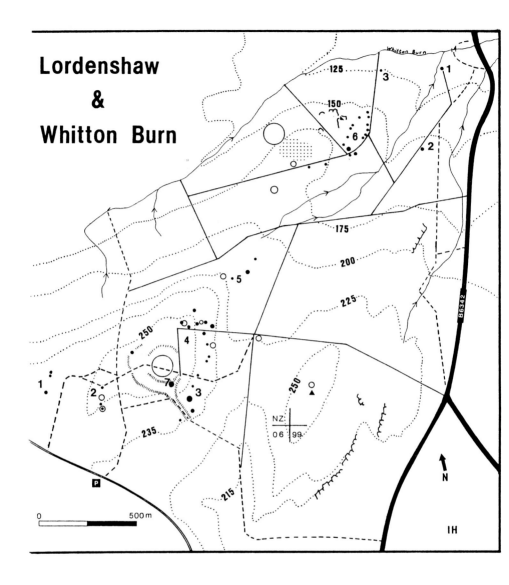

Lordenshaw & Whitton Burn

KEY

Rocks with motifs:

1	.
2-3	•
4-6	●
7-8	⬤

Footpaths   − − −
Contours in metres ·········
Triangulation point ▲

single cairn   ○
multiple cairns   ⦾

hillfort/ settlement ◯
standing stone   ◤
quarry   ▒

South of the Coquet

The south side of the river has its rock art focussed upon Lordenshaw and Garleigh Moor. This area is not the highest, for south are the Simonside Hills, but there is a commanding view from the Lordenshaw hillfort to which the land rises from the Whitton Burn. There are many hollow ways, but although the hill-slopes provide natural routes between stream valleys and to the crossing places of the Coquet, many of these ways are cattle drove tracks and quarry ways.

That the whole valley was important in many Prehistoric periods is attested by the number of hillforts and settlements strung along it. The name Rothbury indicates that in Saxon times it was Hrotha's fortification. Commanding viewpoints there are in plenty, and people have made use of them for centuries.

A marked rock, now lost, but drawn as a slab with four cup marks, came from an excavated large cairn at <u>Ravensheugh</u> <u>(HOO700)</u>, that had a kerb and cist <u>(NZ 017 991)</u>

<u>LORDENSHAW</u> is a much-visited, accessible moorland with excellent views all round. A focal point is an iron age fort, with settlement probably continuing in the Roman period, with an additional 'hollow way' flanked by stone alignments. Parts of what appear to be 'wild' moorland are wide rig-and-furrow ploughed, showing use as arable, resulting in the loss of some earlier monuments.

There are enclosures of different periods, including small shielings and many earth and stone 'dykes' (walls). There are many small standing stones, some parts of walls and other alignments. A few cairns have survived agriculture, and although some may be field clearance, others with cists and kerbs are burial cairns. In this disturbed landscape are rock outcrops, many very extensive, and varied boulders, that have motifs. Much stone has been quarried, with iron tools evident. Lordenshaw has a distinctive style of rock-marking: large cups, some basins, and very long ducts that often spring from basins and cups. The cups and rings are not so elaborate or as aesthetically pleasing as those in north Northumberland. There is a large number of cups, including clusters of 'midget' cups. Although sandstone does weather naturally into ducts on a steep downward slope, some ducts were begun or modified by people. Some basins are natural, but others are used as part of an overall design.

It is almost impossible to see some of the motifs without strong, oblique light, and you may find it difficult in poor conditions to reconcile the drawings with what you see on the rocks. Shallow motifs and lichen cover don't help.

Much of the work on these sites was pioneered by Mr. Newbigin, and this section includes his findings, and more. This is the first extensive survey with accurate drawings to be published, and has taken weeks of work to finalise.

For convenience, the area is divided into 7 sites, with alphabetical sub-sections for individual rocks.

There is sufficient official public access to this area to enable you to visit almost every marked rock. Sites 1-5 can be visited in that order, starting from the minor road along a wide footpath via Birky Hill and ending at the fence that divides pasture from heather. A stile gives access to Site 6 and on to the Whitton Burn group, but these sites can also be reached from the Hexham-Rothbury road at the stone bridge.
H00680. NZ 0512 9912. WEST LORDENSHAW (BIRKY HILL),1, a-e.
Birky Hill is the small hill and ridge that marks the western edge of the area of rock motifs, before the land slopes away to the Whitton Burn. The hill has a ruined cairn or enclosure.
Outcrop rocks a,b,c are on the hill itself, two prominent and one near horizontal. The cup and rings on (a) are faint. On (b) a natural basin has been utilized. Linear arrangements of cups are a feature of (c).
The famous, complex pattern on the 'Horseshoe Rock'(d), NZ 0502 9918, with its spectacular views right through to the Cheviot range, is one of the best in the county.
(e) is 20 metres north of the Horseshoe.

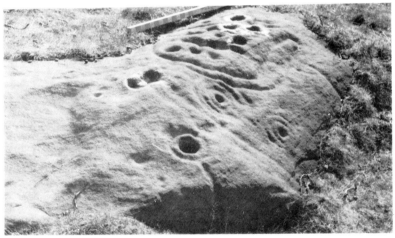

1d

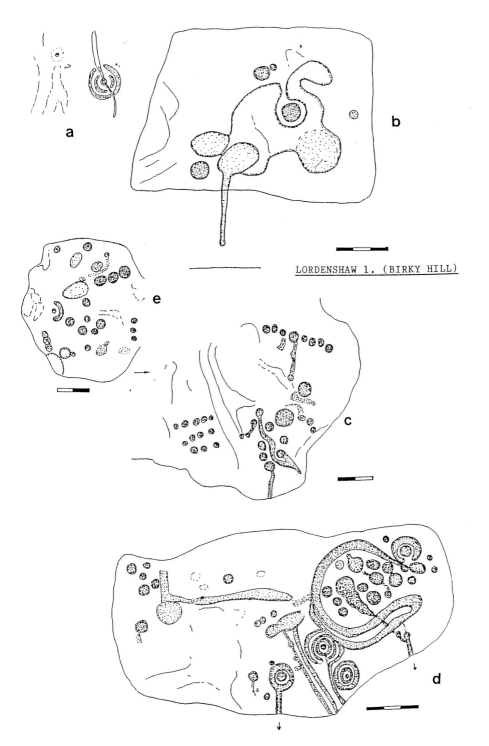

LORDENSHAW 1. (BIRKY HILL)

H00681.   NZ 0524 9916. WEST LORDENSHAW. 2,a-f.
Beginning at the south, the rocks are:
(a) At NZ 0525 9905, a small round cairn, robbed, and now crescent-shaped, with 2 contiguous cup-marked boulders.
(b) 23m. away from (a) at 34 degrees is a thin, triangular-shaped standing stone with cups.
(c) After passing another mound (20m. away), a further 39m. brings you to the main rock, with a cup and ring on the same outcrop 11m away at a lower level.
(d) 148m (60 deg.) in a line across the remains of a shieling enclosure is a near-vertical rock in an earth wall.
(e) is 50m. from (d) at a lower level in the field wall.

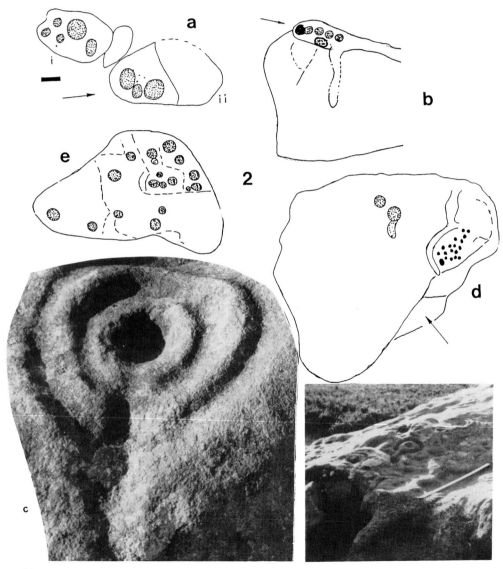

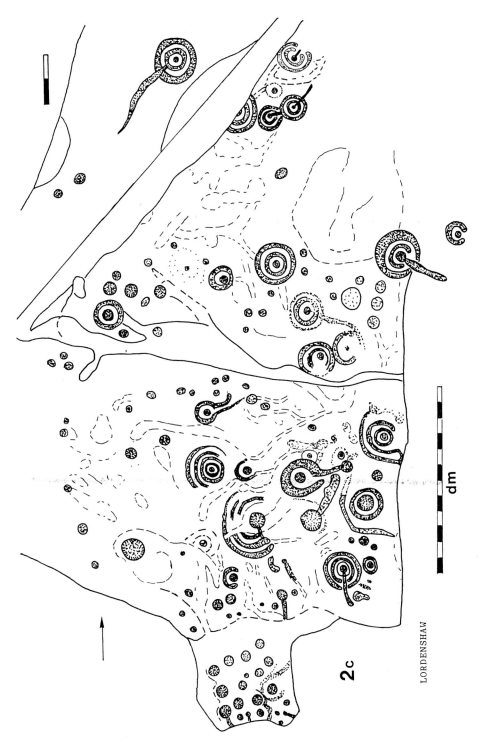

2c

LORDENSHAW

dm

25

HOO682. NZ 0562 9909 to 0565 9935. EAST LORDENSHAW. 3 a-r.
A hollow way leads from the south to the interior of the
hillfort. Among the scatter of standing/ aligned stones are 3
with markings (a-c). About 30m west of the hollow way, a
series of marked rocks begins. They lie on the eastern slope
of the hill. Rocks (d)- (f) are close together and ascend the
slope in that order.
(g) is cup-marked, (h) is a group of rocks with 'basins' that
are natural, (i) is a sloping outcrop with cups at the head and
a long duct, and (j) and (k) lie above it. North is an outcrop
with some cups (l). Then there is an earthen field wall, a
clear area in grass overlying rig and furrow, to the north.
(m) is high up the slope towards the hill fort, with cups and
one ring, (n) lies east of it above a small mound: a long duct
may be natural. (o) is 3m from (m), but the cups reported by
Newbigin are obscured.(p) lies east of a small mound on the
downward slope. and (q) is the most interesting of all: a near-
horizontal rock   lavishly   stippled with 'midget' cups, and
carrying on its near-horizontal surface a large basin
surrounded by a groove, linked cups, and cup and ring.
The deer park wall that has cut into the eastern outer rampart
of the hillfort is joined by a wall from the SE, which ends
this series with (r), a small marked rock between wall and (q).

HOO683. NZ 0569 9938 to 0565 9950. EAST LORDENSHAW 4.(a)-(o)
This group of rock outcrops includes one of the largest sloping
outcrops, very long man-made grooves, and cups on the outcrop
on which round barrows have been built. It lies just east of
the ridge that forms the natural trackway that leads from the
Whitton Burn to the hillfort.
NZ 0569 9938 (a)-(d) are four parts of the same outcrop that
stands out not only in length and height, but in the size and
depth of its cups and ducts.
(e) lies to the north, with many ducts and the addition
stylistically of linked cups and rings. (f), with cups and
rings is narrowly split from it to the north.
(g) lies up the slope to the west, where a long outcrop has cup
marks.
There is a prominent disturbed barrow at NZ 0557 9942, with
two stones in part of an alignment , (h) and (i) between it and
an earth wall to the south. The barrow has two cup- marked
blocks, (j,k), built into it on the east kerb, and (l) is a
small rounded boulder in the disturbed centre. From this
barrow the land slopes towards the Whitton Burn, and down to NZ
0565 9950, three minor rocks (m-o) carry markings.

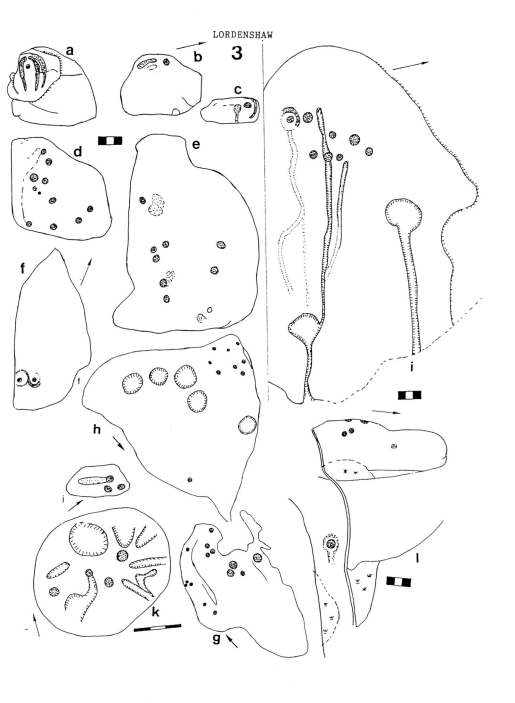

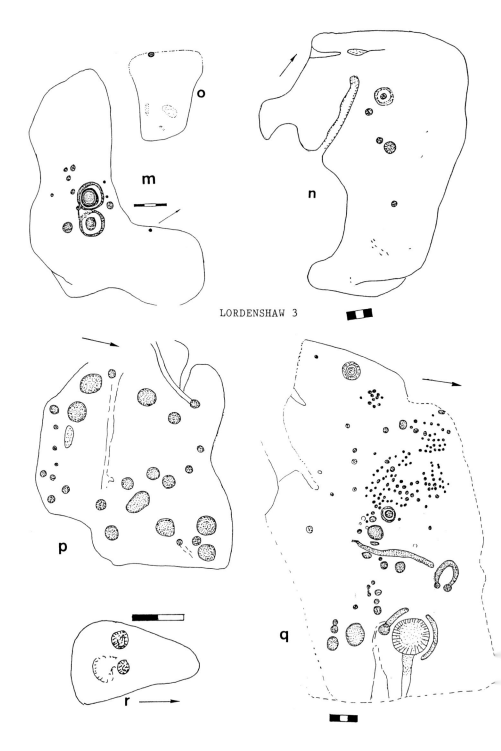

LORDENSHAW 3

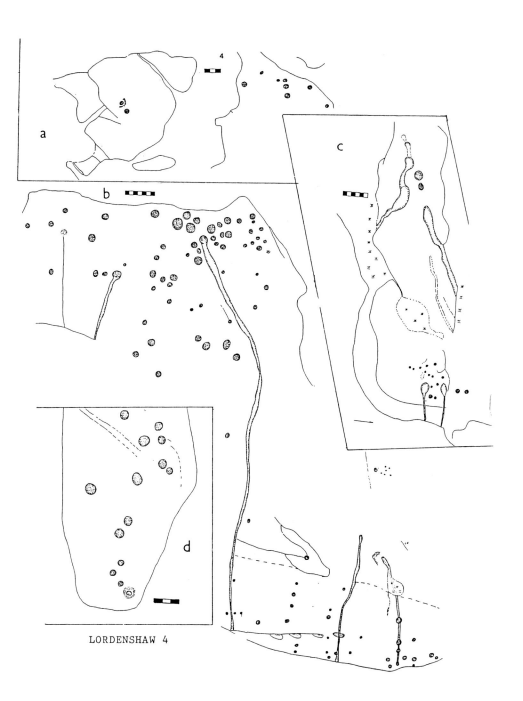

a

b

c

d

LORDENSHAW 4

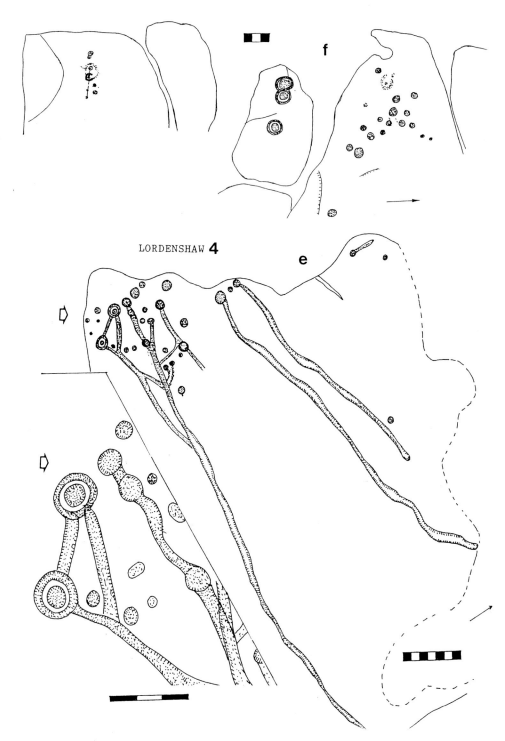

LORDENSHAW **4**

f

e

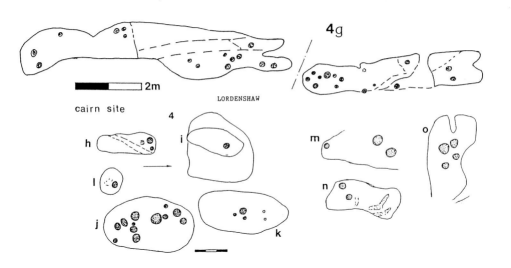

4g

LORDENSHAW

cairn site   4

h   i   m   o

l   n

j   k

cist

H00684. NZ 0578 9960 to 0586 9969.   EAST LORDENSHAW 5. (a)-(h)
This group leads downhill towards the Whitton Burn. The remains
of an excavated round burial cairn, containing still-visible
large and small cists is the starting point.
(a) is a large marked outcrop rock to the east, 18m. away. NE,
across a track and hollow way is a series of smaller outcrops
with markings, ending with a large outcrop.
(b) is 79m from (a) bearing 234 degrees, (c) is 83m., and (d)
is 102m. from (a), the latter being an overhang rock that is
7m, via (e),(f) and (g) to (h). Rock (h) is on a bearing of 230
degrees to 5(a).   There are other faint single cup marks on
other stones in the area.

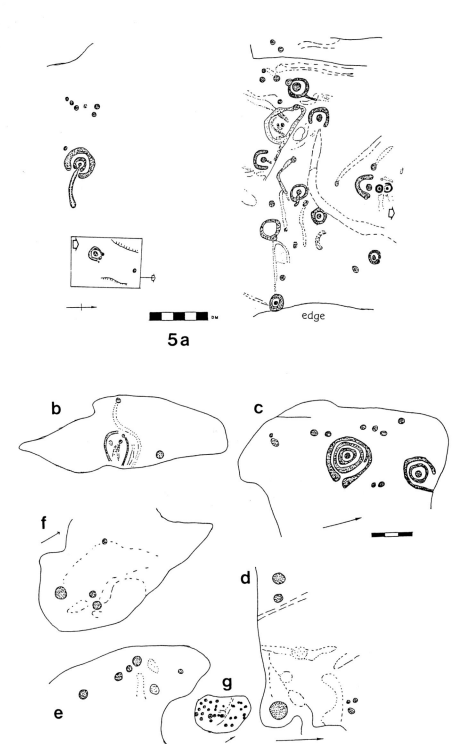

5a

edge

b

c

f

d

e

g

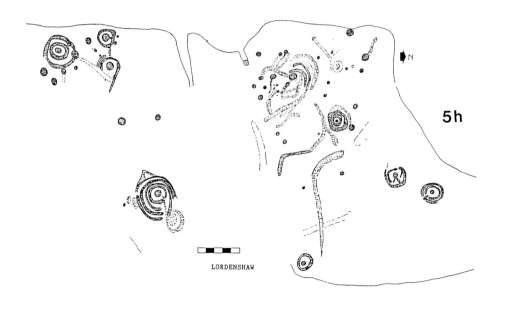

LORDENSHAW

5h

H00685. NZ0595 9995 to 0640 0050. EAST LORDENSHAW 6.
This is an area that includes a small settlement to the west,
(NZ 0595 0015), cairns, standing stone, and a wide use of rock
surfaces for cups and rings and, more dramatically, some very
long ducts. The latter incorporate cups and rings at the
starting place of the ducts.
(a) From site 5, a fence divides heather from grassland, and
two stiles cross to it. Ahead is a wall built in one place
over a small outcrop, the highest between sites 5 and 6, that
has pick-marked (fresh) motifs. A burial cairn lies c. 50m. SW
from it.   (b) is on the next ridge towards the Whitton Burn,
facing the burn on the down slope, where there is a number of
outcrops, some quarried. This one, 10m. from the wall, is cup-
marked.
(c) is outcrop on a quarry edge where two fences and walling
join precariously on it, by a green path heading towards the
burn.   Rocks (c)-(f) all lie east of the fence within a few
metres of one another.
(g) lies north of the wall junctions, (h) is on a knoll, (i) is
an outcrop with a small mound (quarry upcast or cairn?) on
top, and is one of the most interesting in the area. Two deep
cups appear on the outcrop below the mound.
(j) is a large outcrop that is close to the earthen wall that
runs downhill to the burn.   (k) and (l) are boulders that form
part of an alignment of small stones, (m) is outcrop above a
quarried area that has one cup mark (not drawn) among its
dislodged stones.

The northern limit of Site 6 is marked by outcrop rock that has large ducts.   (n) is a cup-marked boulder 10m. east of (o), which has a large duct and cups. (p) has multiple ducts that are grassed over towards the end of the slope.

(q) lies on a western outcrop edge, and (r), (s), (t) are minor cup-marks at the limit of their appearance.

(u) is the area south of the wall, where there are some large irregular cup/basin shapes, some of which seem to be natural.

There are many surface irregularities caused by quarrying and the making of field walls, and there is the added complication for the unwary that some features belong to the old golf course.

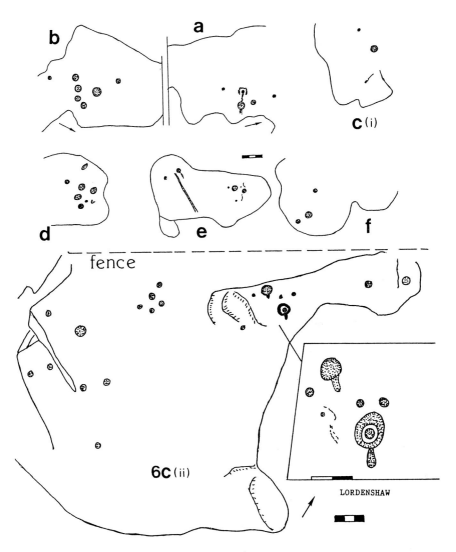

b

a

c (i)

d

e

f

fence

6c (ii)

LORDENSHAW

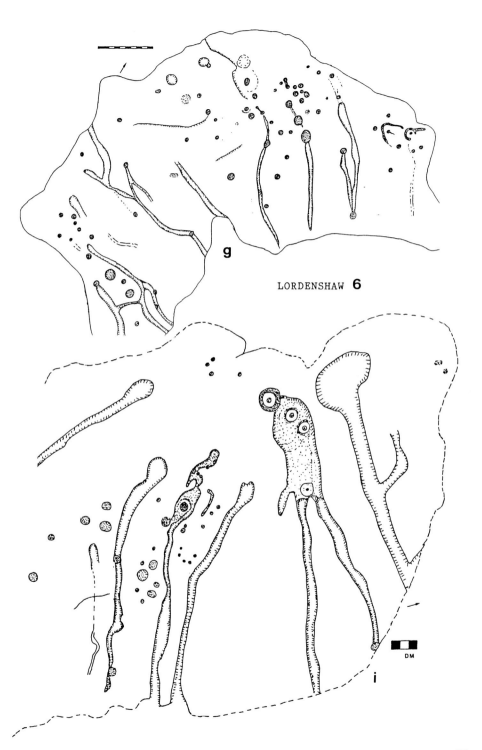

LORDENSHAW 6

g

i

DM

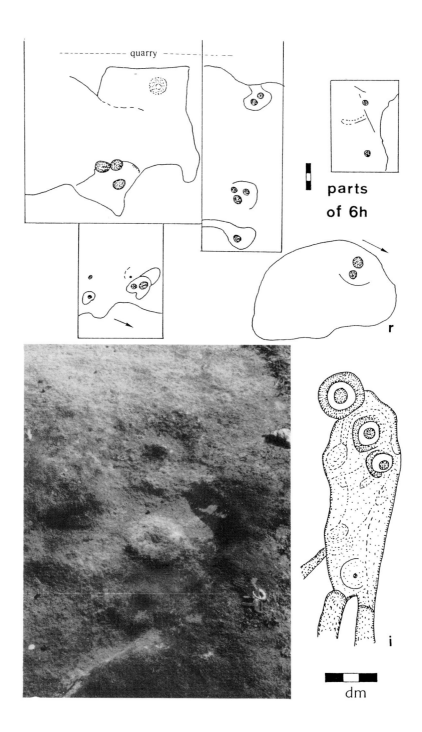

quarry

parts
of 6h

r

i

dm

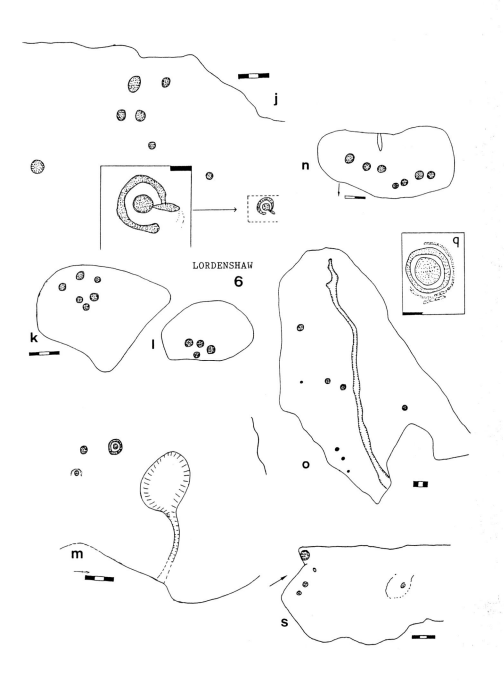

LORDENSHAW

6

The hillfort that occupies the top of Lordenshaw has been
modified many times.   Part of the rampart and ditch at the
south has been turned into a settlement of hut circles and
small enclosures, and a deep hollow way leads into it, flanked
by large stones.   Field walls of later enclosures focus on the
whole complex.

To the west of the entry of the hollow way into the settlement
are outcrops, some quarried, and some of these are cup-marked.
The most northerly,(a),is on the edge of the rampart, 16m.south
of the east entrance.   Five others on the east edge of an
enclosure are lettered b-f, from N-S.   (b) is 14m from the
rampart, and the others follow in distances from each other:
(c) 7m, (d) 14m, (e) 8m, and (f) 3m.   The marks are faint.

Lordenshaw (which may mean lower stream wood), has attracted
human activity for thousands of years, beginning with the
commanding position itself within the total landscape, through
its use as a burial and religious site, possibly with stone
alignments, then as a defence, a settlement, a Deer Park,
pasture and arable, and now as marginal pasture and tourist
attraction.

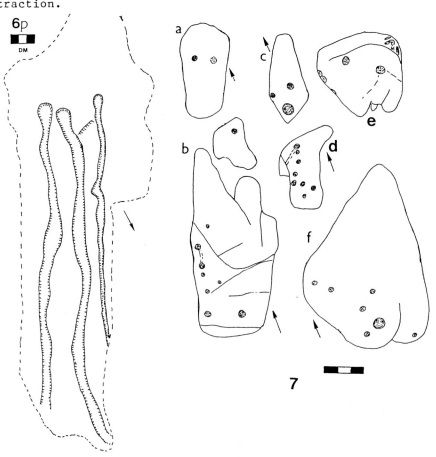

6p

DM

a

c

e

b

d

f

7

2c

WHITTON BURN SITES

The sites are a continuation of Lordenshaw 6, but can best be reached from the Hexham-Rothbury road, where there is parking space by a gate that leads to the Whitton Burn bridge.

H00686. NZ 0660 0045 WHITTON BURN 1,(a) and (b).

Two rocks lie, exceptionally, in a narrow stream valley, on a ridge flanked on the E. by a hollow way and W. by a feeder of the Whitton Burn. (a) lies W. of a fence with barbed wire, under trees. (b): this detached block of sandstone with its single cup lies opposite (a) among other apparently disturbed blocks under a hawthorn tree. Southwards, the land rises towards Lordenshaw, via a large clump of gorse bushes. A triangle formed by the junction of a wire fence on stone and earth and an earthen wall is where the next site is:-

H00687   NZ 0655 0013, WHITTON BURN 2, (a),(b),and (c).

The area has been quarried, and burial mounds have been removed from it, but on remaining outcrops are :

(a) 5m. from the west fence, cups and rings with one cup and ring completely 'fresh'

(b) is 8m. SSE of (a), and (c) is on the same outcrop, 10m. S. of (a).

H00688   NZ 0640 0042. WHITTON BURN 3. The site is reached from the bridge to a field gate beside the burn.East of an earthen wall is a dome of rock with cup marks. South of it, uphill, are the sites of Lordenshaw 6.

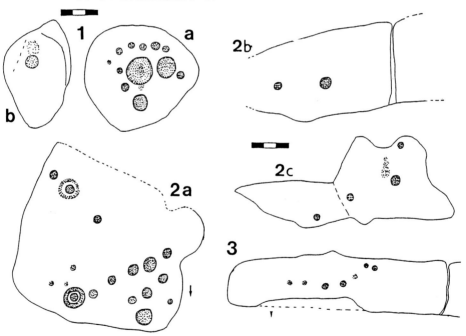

From Whitton Burn and Addeyheugh to Millstone Burn
===
At Debdon Whitefield, a marked stone on the kerb of a <u>barrow</u>
(HO0660. NU 076 036), with 27 small cups and two grooves, was
found, but the stretch of moorland between the Rothbury area
and Millstone Burn has not yet revealed other motifs where one
might expect them to be!
However, there is certainly a Prehistoric link between the two
areas, in the form of single cairns and cairnfields, a field
system, a small village of stone-based hut circles, and
standing stones (mostly small). It is an area where, if any
change is made to the vegetation, rigorous field work will have
to be carried out. It is highly likely that what we see is an
area at least used as a routeway, and by some as a settlement
area (perhaps Iron Age in the case of the 'village'). Evidence
at the Cragside end lies under Lord Armstrong's re-landscaping
of the moor.
HO0661. Pauperhaugh Farm: NU 101 997 approx. a cup mark stone
was reported 'near the mouth of the Black Burn', but cannot be
traced.

MILLSTONE BURN (some access, but some private)

The swathe of marked rock that seems to pick up from
Lordenshaw, Whitton Burn and Cartington Moor, slopes into the
Burn and re-appears on Snook Bank. There are prominent
outcrops that have been quarried, wide views from every
outcrop, bellpits, hollow ways connected with quarrying, coal
extraction, and with an iron bloomery site. The Roman Devil's
Causeway is still visible, with its flat road surface and
flanking ditches, moving in a different direction from the
Prehistoric route that the motifs suggest. In places the land
has been cleared of all small stone, and heather grows
compactly, and on the south side of the boundary fence is
untidy ground, with thistles, nettles, and marsh grass.
Through all this the marked surfaces of outcrop rocks appear,
for a while following the RDC boundary, then fanning out
towards the Coquet and Corby Crags. It is a wide expanse of
country that is marked in this way, with the line of the Fell
sandstone scarp and the 'hoe' down to the Coquet valley
flanking it.
There are no settlement sites, but there are occasional burial
cairns and flints. The overall impression is that this is
territory for nomads, but one would have to be sure that the
vegetation has not radically altered since the motifs were put
there. The Debdon Whitefield sites indicate some sort of
settlement, for example, including field systems.
All the marked rocks appear below as drawings, with site
numbers. Some have been lost in land drainage recently, and
others can soon become overgrown and temporarily 'lost'.
SITE 1: HO0645 (No. 1 on the plan is NU 1189 0521)
These lie in a triangular-shaped field east of the road, and
the portables, found by Bob Robson, are in Berwick Museum,
(HO0704, a and b).

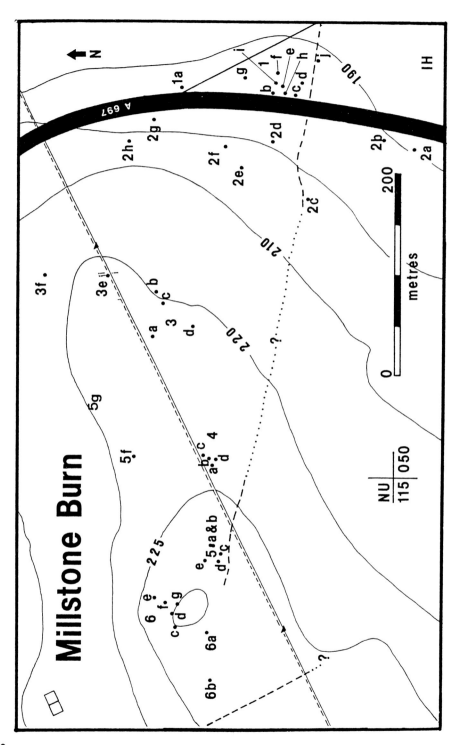

Millstone Burn

SITE 2: HOO646. (2h is NU 1184 0525).
These are all on land from the road to the top of the slope.
SITE 3: HOO647 (3b is NU 1160 0523).
These are grouped on either side of the boundary fence, east.
SITE 4: HOO648 (NU 1151 0517)
This site is focussed on a large outcrop that includes a deep
square slot that may have been intended for something like a
cross.
SITE 5: HOO649 (5a is NU 1143 0519).
North of the boundary fence
SITE 6: HOO650 (6d is NU 1142 0528).
On and above the crag edge, before the land slopes away. Apart
from some isolated cups, this marks the limit of the motifs.

MILLSTONE BURN SITE 1

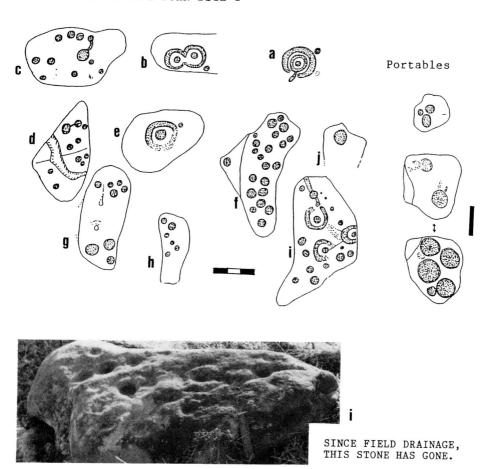

Portables

i

SINCE FIELD DRAINAGE,
THIS STONE HAS GONE.

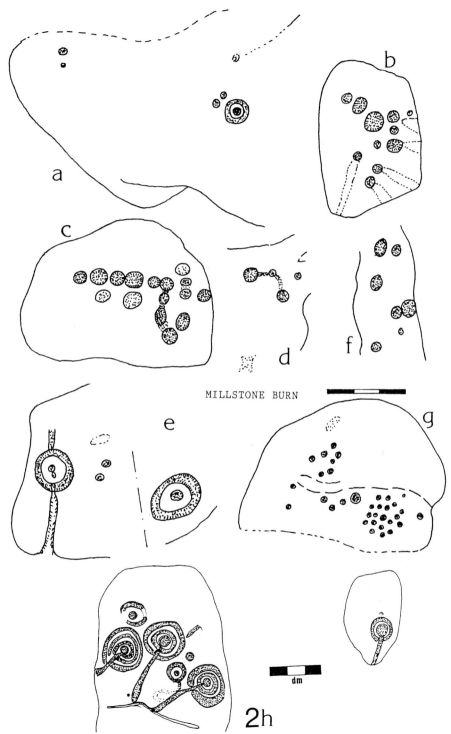

MILLSTONE BURN

2h

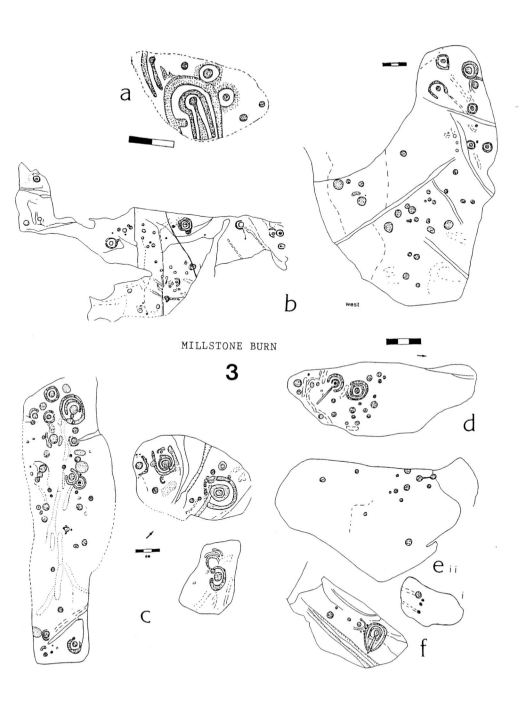

MILLSTONE BURN

3

west

a

b

c

d

e ii
i

f

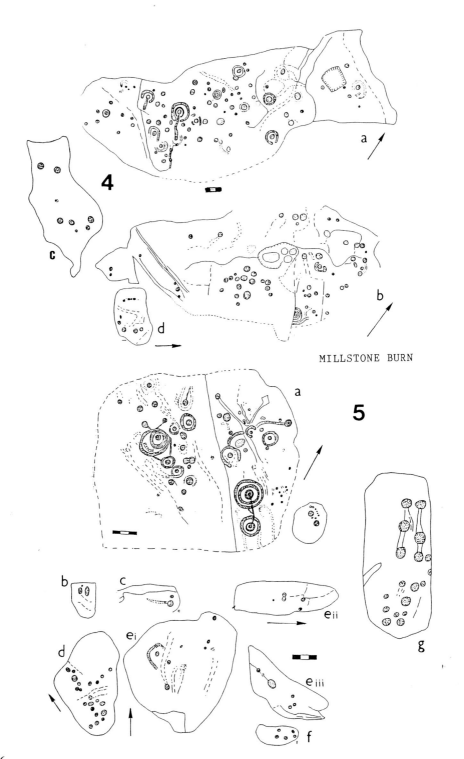

MILLSTONE BURN

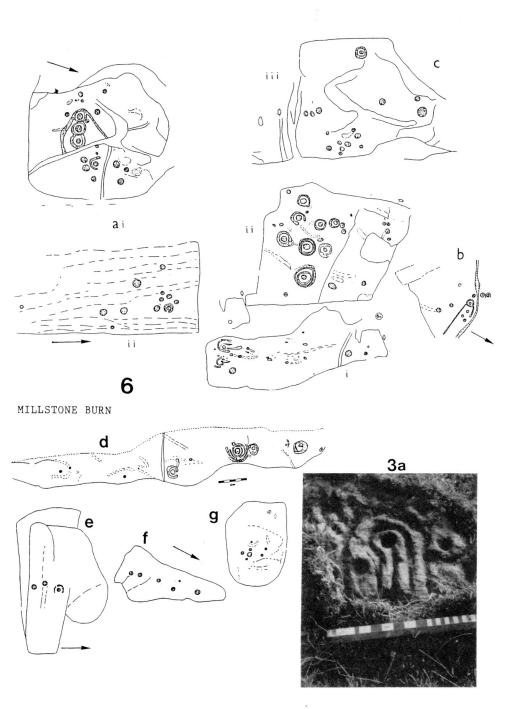

a i

i i

i i i

c

i i

b

i

6

MILLSTONE BURN

d

e

f

g

3a

<u>NU 1274 0543 SNOOK BANK</u> (Footpath, but permission needed for extensive search)
Snook Bank has a most intriguing origin: 'Schakelzerdesnoke' in 1264, it means the shackle yard where cattle were tied on a projecting piece of land. The views from marked rocks are extensive. The land is enclosed, upland pasture, with outcrop rocks quarried for stone, including millstones (one spoiled , still in situ). Some of these motifs are reported here for the first time.
<u>Site 1. H00652.</u> <u>NU 1293 0520</u>: in the field that includes deep rigs close to the farm, and a partly walled 'garden'- a disused enclosure. Three rocks include a possible standing stone (c) with a cup mark on top.
<u>Site 2. H00653.</u> <u>NU 1290 0530</u>: between a wire fence and steep outcrop on a minor outcrop ridge.
<u>Site 3. H00654.</u> <u>NU 1276 0544</u>: a rectangular block, flush with the ground, with 'pecking' clear, 50m. due south of the cliff site 4. 8m. east is a possible cairn, of small cobbles.
<u>Site 4. H00655.</u> <u>NU 1277 0541</u>: a major site on the rock slopes south. There are 2 main areas, and some scattered marks.
<u>Site 5. H00656.</u> NU 126 056: contained within a large triangular area, two sides of which are walls and boundary stones. Some unrecorded cairns lie west of the NE wall, the largest 4m. diameter, with its centre dug into. There are scattered cup marks, which have grown over, and a cup and ring stone that lay at the centre of a dug-out mound cannot now be traced.
<u>Site 6. H00657</u> is a large area where small quarries in rough ground give way to pasture before the land falls away to the Millstone Burn. There are 6 small cairns (clearance?) on the edge of pasture, and one (possibly more) in it, and this is where the motifs are. Rows of stone blocks marked 'W.D.' will help you to find the rocks, which begin with 4 cups on a standing stone next to the last of the WD blocks.
(a) NU 1252 0551, (b) NU 1250 0544, (c) NU 1250 0540,
(d) NU 1254 0545, (e) NU 1245 0546, (f) 3 minor outcrops with some cups are at NU 1246 0547, (g) is on quarried outcrop, and (h) lies close to a clearance mound at the SW of the pasture. The drawings, recording these rocks for the first time, show that some parts of the motifs are freshly peck-marked, whilst others appear smoothed and deepened. Away from the sites on lower land to the south is a kerbed cairn, found by P.Dwyer.

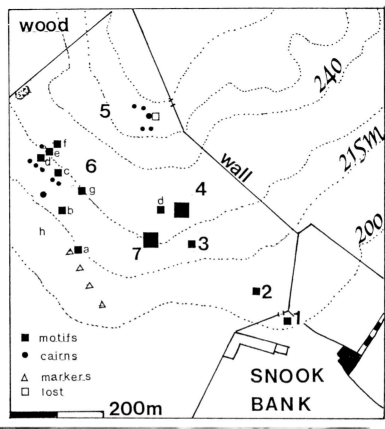

wood

240

215m

5

wall

6

4

200

7

3

2

1

■ motifs
● cairns
△ markers
□ lost

200m

SNOOK
BANK

6d

Site 7. HO0658. NU 1264 0434
Promontories of rock, facing SSW, form a
millstone quarry. 7(a) still has a
roughed-out millstone in situ, and the
motifs on this rock lie on the east and
west of the northern end.
7(a) is due east of 6(a), and SW of 7(b)
and 4. The motifs are deep.

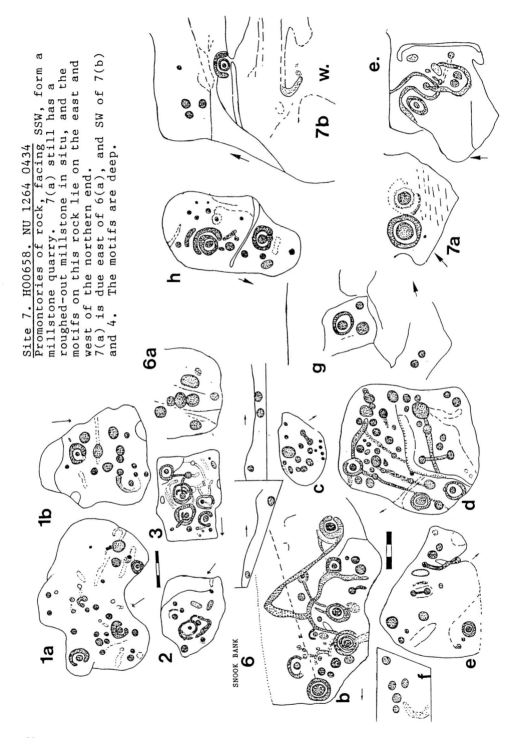

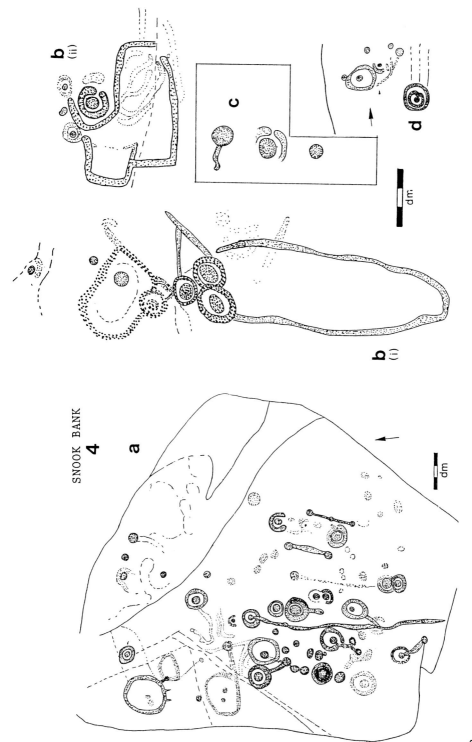

SNOOK BANK

4

a

b (i)

b (ii)

c

d

dm

dm

51

H00651.   NU 1150 0695.   CALLER CRAG (accessible)
On a vertical cliff face, facing a fairly level area where
there are at least two burial cairns, one with a disturbed
cist,and overlooking a level stretch of land before the next
scarp drop, there are many well-defined cups.   There is also a
flat-bottomed standing stone with natural cup-like hollows,on
outcrop. The name means ' the calf crag'.

H00644.   NU 1279 0962.   CORBY CRAGS (accessible).
On the top surface of this domed rock-shelter is a basin and
groove design, with a large duct.   On the floor is a long,
curved groove made with a stone pick (distinguishable from
later iron marks).   The   floor that I excavated revealed
material from Mesolithic to the present day, and a cremation in
an enlarged food vessel under a triangular-shaped stone.   The
connection between Early Bronze Age burial and the motifs is
highly probable.   Nearby is a standing stone and an Iron Age
enclosure.
A 'corby' is a crow.

H00643.   NU 1294 1080.   LEMMINGTON WOOD (private wood).
This site is very difficult to find, and was relocated recently
by Irene and Ian Hewitt who, in clearing the rock, discovered
the runes that are included here.   The latter are unique in the
area, and one wonders whether they were deliberately put there
because of a much earlier symbolism.   It is impossible to say.
The name means settlement where brooklime (Speedwell) grows.

H00642.   NU 1380 1125.   LAMP HILL (accessible).
On the highest point of outcrop crag, among some quarry marks,
is a cup, and a domino pattern of six small cups.   The latter
makes use of a natural rectangular depression.

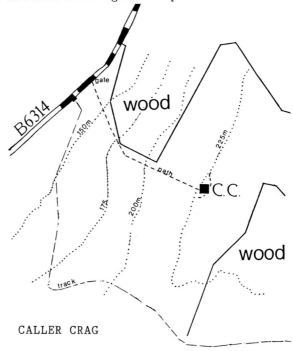

CALLER CRAG

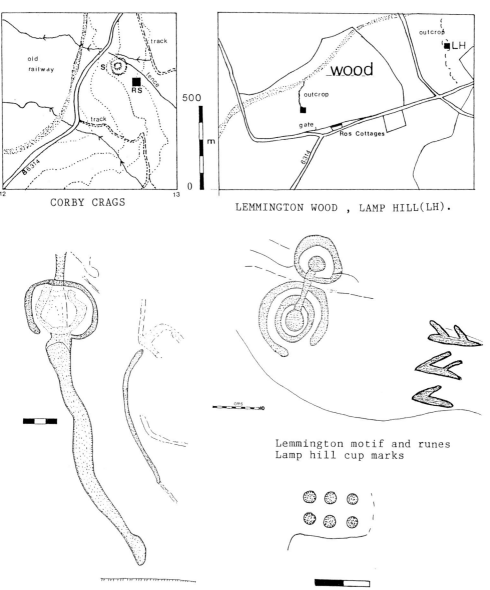

CORBY CRAGS

LEMMINGTON WOOD , LAMP HILL(LH).

Lemmington motif and runes
Lamp hill cup marks

CORBY CRAGS ROCK SHELTER
Left: top of rock
Right: rock shelter floor.

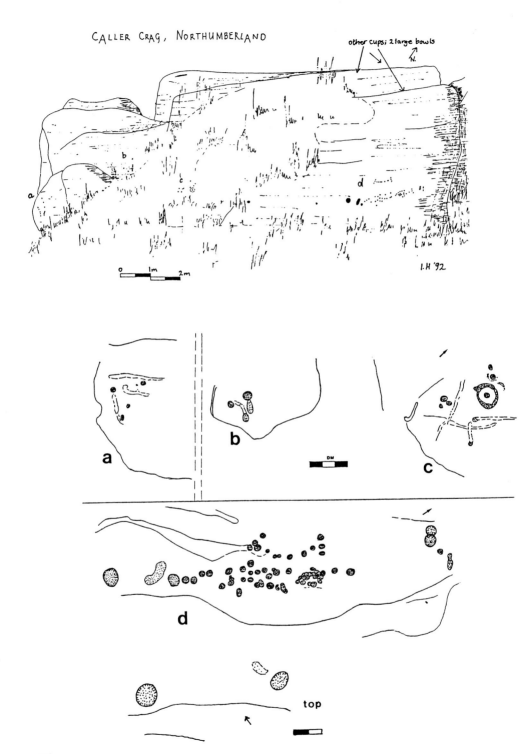

CALLER CRAG, NORTHUMBERLAND

other cups; 2 large bowls

N.

a

b

c

d

0   1m   2m

I.H '92

a

b

DM

c

d

top

This sandstone cliff rising from the River Coquet at a fording place is a superb example of a 'special' place, that, for reasons unknown to us, became a focus of ritual attention. Spiral designs occur only on one other local rock: at Lilburn. As we see in Cumbria, these motifs are usually in the west. They also occur on a vertical face, whereas the bulk of motifs are on near-horizontal surfaces.

The horned spirals, triple spirals, and running spirals form a unique group in Britain. Some lie at flood water level, but others cannot be reached without a ladder.

The markings occur in two groups, separated by jutting rock. No.1 is at the east end (a-f), and are the easiest reached, but to reach the next group, 2,(a-f), you have to duck under the rock overhang, to the west. To return to Morwick Mill from there is difficult along the cliff edge of the river.

Two enclaves are thus formed naturally, separated by jutting rock, and there is nothing to link place with settlement or time. Drawings best describe them, and establish their unique place in Northumberland's rock art. They are not variations on a theme, but are a different concept.

Morwick means 'fen farm'.

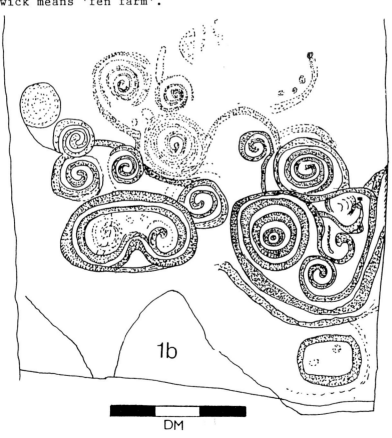

1b

DM

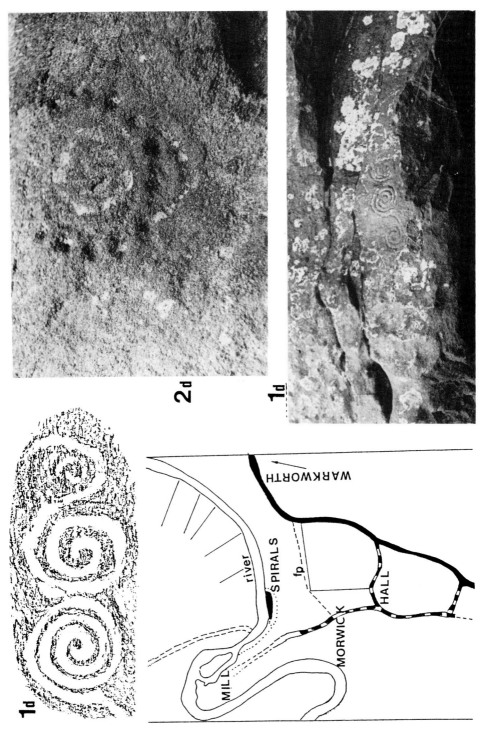

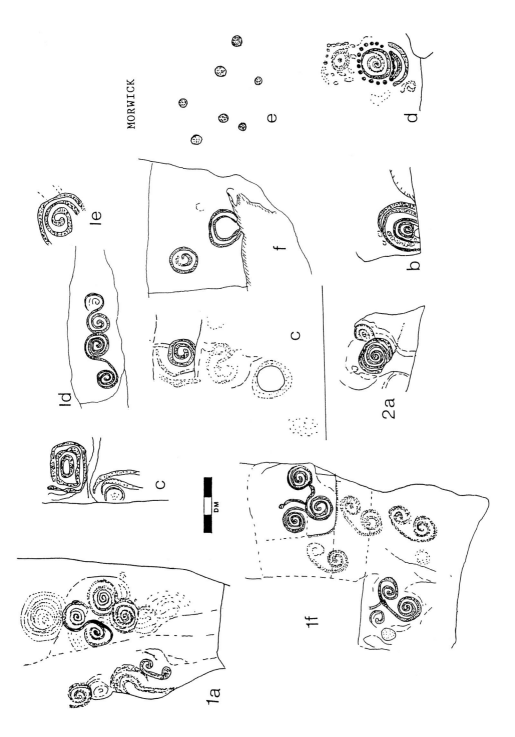

MORWICK

Into this region are placed the rest of Northumberland's marked
rocks, many of which are very recent discoveries.
H00761.   NY 9720 8913.   TOD CRAG, OTTERCOPS MOSS.(Accessible)
This large outcrop at the end of a plantation has motifs that
appear to have been put there at different times, with an arc
of double rings around cups being predominant.

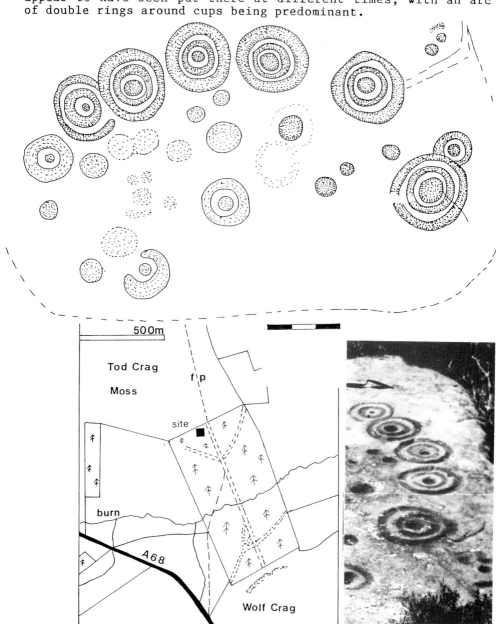

HOO759. NY 8208 9210. PADON HILL.(Access).
West of the Pennine Way fence is outcrop rock, north of Grey
Mare, with clear cup marks, reported by Harry Rowland.
HOO760. NY 828 914.   WHITELY PIKE, NORTH SUNDAY SIGHT.(5
small boulders or outcrops).
This site on a boulder-strewn moor of outcrop sandstone was
first recorded by R.Charlton. The small markings are different
from the usual, for they are recessed dish- or small basin-
shaped. They are not unprecedented, but it is unusual to have
only this type in one area. They were first reported in
'Redewetter', 1983, an occasional publication of the Redesdale
Society, by R. Charlton, and drawn there by Diane Charlton. A
cist was also found in the vicinity.
HOO762. NY 828 844. REENES FARM(now at Hesleyside)
This formed part of a stone 'dyke'(wall) that had fallen down.
HOO763. NY 887 793. PITLAND HILLS BARROW, BIRTLEY
This is one of the most important sites, because 17 marked
stones, varying in shape and size, came from a large burial
mound with two cists, a food vessel and cinerary urn
asociation. The marked rocks were not uprooted or broken
outcrop rock, but small cobble-type sandstones.
HOO764. NY 851 791 HOUXTY COTTAGE(accessible).
Martin Sumner was the first to see this well-executed motif in
the outside kitchen wall of Houxty Cottage.

NORTH SUNDAY SIGHT

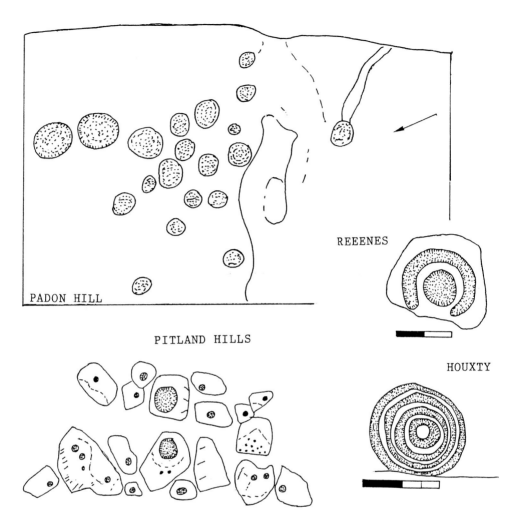

REEENES

PADON HILL

PITLAND HILLS

HOUXTY

H00701. NY 0485 9530 BLUEBURN FARM
This portable, deep cup-marked stone may be prehistoric, and
has no context. It is at Newcastle.
FONTBURN RESERVOIR GROUP.
The four marked rocks are spread out on either side of the
Fallowlees Burn, in an area of enclosures and barrows,(circles
with C and E on map).
(a) NZ 0223 9379 measures 2m.x 1.5m. on which surface are at
least 6 well-defined cups, but I have not seen it, as it has
been covered over.
(b) NZ 0327 9330 is a large erratic block of sandstone,
comparable to that at Old Bewick, standing at the corner of a
plantation in what would have commanded a wide view of the
valley, but for trees.
(c) NZ 0324 9366 is a four-poster stone circle with cups and
faint ring on the N.stone(c ii), and cups on the E.stone(c i).

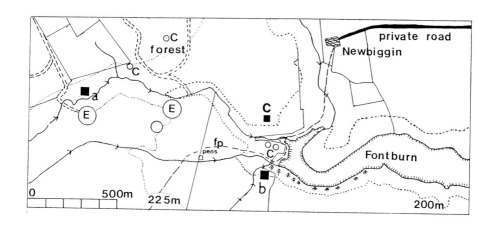

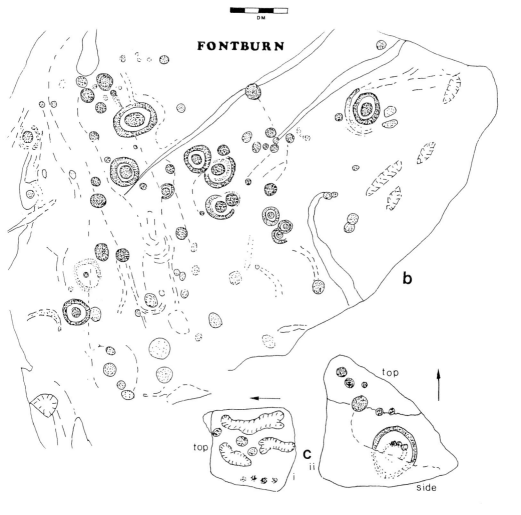

FONTBURN

b

c

i

ii

top

side

top

61

H00751.   NZ 0330 8350. OLD DEANHAM. 6 portables (a)-(f)
Thanks to the work of John Davies, and the owner, Chris Whaley,
outstanding portables have been found on a site that has been
extensively farmed, as wide rig and furrow testifies.
The contexts, in old field walls, indicate   field clearance.
Such small cobbles are extensively worked on one or two
surfaces, suggesting a special use as portables.
(c) shows signs of a two-stage design: the inset shows the
earlier 'pecking' marks.
H00741.   NZ 008 853   THE FAWNS,   KIRKWHELPINGTON
A slab with a cup mark provided a base for an inverted
cinerary urn.   Now at the British Museum.
H00742.   ?   CAMBO WALLINGTON AREA.
The Rev. Rome Hall reported a 23cm. x 8cm. stone with a single
cup mark, but it has gone.

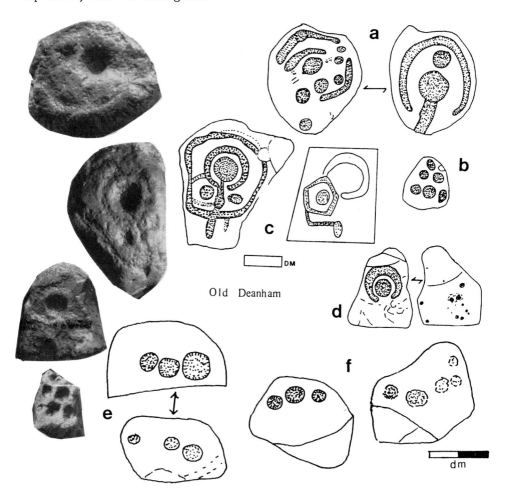

Old   Deanham

62

Until recently, no motifs had been discovered on the Shaftoe-Bolam outcrops, but the work of John Davies, helped by farmers R.Leaper, the Keegan brothers, Major Hedley-Dent and W.Robson has brought some to light. Shaftoe means shaft-shaped ridge.

H00752.   NZ 0587 8395 MIDDLETON BANK TOP. (Public footpath).

These motifs, on a long, thin outcrop, with extensive views, lie among field systems and cairns.

H00754.   NZ 0530 8355.   SHAFTOE CRAG, JUBILEE MEMORIAL SITE.

Prominent on Shaftoe Crag, north of an Iron Age enclosure, is a natural platform of outcrop rock, quarried vertically on the north.

a) 10.3m.from the Memorial 204 degrees SW, is a faint cup and part ring.

b) 8m. bearing 32 degrees E. of N. from the Memorial is a long groove that originates in cups and rings. The views are great.

H00753.   NZ 043817. WEST SHAFTOE FARM (private)

There are slightly damaged cups and rings on outcrop.

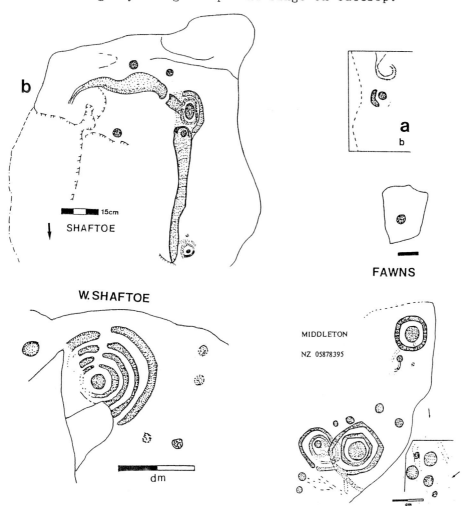

H00787.   NT 079810   SHORTFLATT (a)-(d)

A 'flat' is a name given to a medieval field strip division. The rig and furrow from such land remained visible under pasture until it was recently ploughed again for arable, and the four rocks have come to light in fields dominated by a huge, unexcavated burial mound on a ridge.

a) Now in the wall of Shortflatt Tower in a purpose-built niche.

b) Found in a quarry in the same field as (a), a small portable. (NT 082807)

c) Found in November, 1991.

d) Found in the next field east in January, 1992, again by Bill Robson.

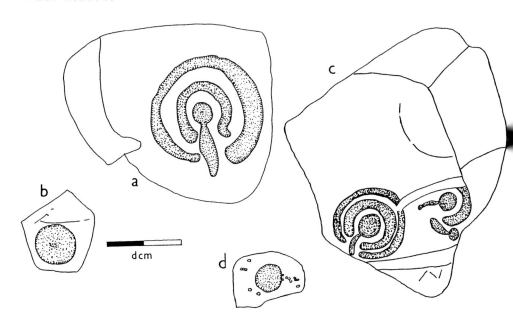

INGOE means Inga's ridge, which gives extensive views. Three marked rocks are listed, the Warrior standing stone being the only one in its context.

H00755.   NZ 043 759. In a garden at Sandyway Heads, this block, marked on two faces, was removed from a field nearby.

H00756   NZ 044 747. Cup- marked standing stone (Warrior Stone).

H00757.   NZ 037 748. A slab, found in a wall, thought by Greenwell to come from a cist, and now in Alnwick Castle.

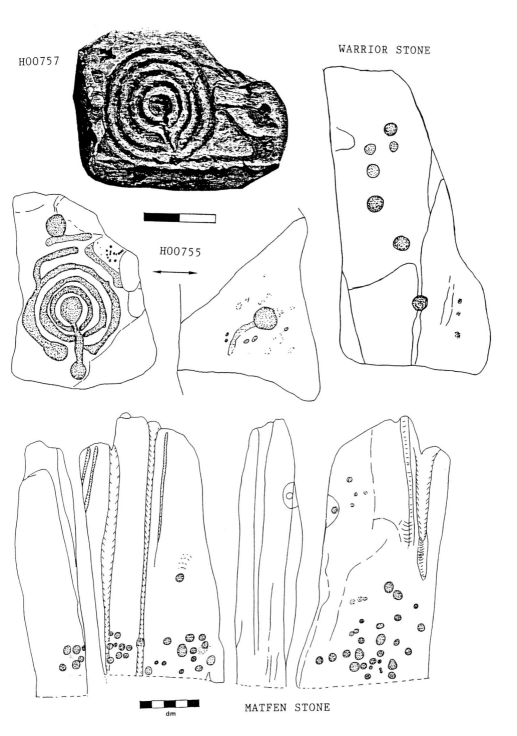

H00757

WARRIOR STONE

H00755

MATFEN STONE

dm

65

H00744.   NZ 032 705.   MATFEN STANDING STONE.
This very interesting, accessible stone on the roadside, has a profusion of cup marks near its base.   It was moved from a field.
H00745.   NZ 084 752.   BLACK HEDDON AREA, (a-d).
Although there is nothing to be seen now on the ground, Tate, Greenwell and Bruce reported many stones associated with burials.   These included cup stones over cremations in a barrow, a cup and ring marked cist with a cremation urn, and cup marked stones over cremations.   Such stones have apparently been lost, and their location (South Moor is mentioned) is only general.
A stone in Newcastle Museum is the only one illustrated, and is provenanced as Stamfordham.

THE OUSTON CAIRN STONE, PIKE HILL, IS IN NEWCASTLE MUSEUM.

HOO749.   NZ 0774 7048. OUSTON, PIKE HILL.
A marked slab with an unusual design came from a burial mound
and cist context, and is at Newcastle. A single cup- marked
slab from inside one of two cists cannot now be traced.
THE RYTON AREA.   Outside Northumberland County.
All stones have been moved. The largest and first on my list is
accessible at Newcastle, but the rest are just for the record.
HOO802.   NZ 1475 3650.   An extensively marked boulder.
HOO803.   NZ 1480 6470.   3 cups on a stone fragment.
HOO804.   NZ 1454 6349.   Cup marked stone.
HOO805.   NZ 1420 6470.   Cup marked stone.
Mr. W.A.Cocks noted other prehistoric material in these areas.
HOO806.   NZ 149 667.   THROCKLEY BANK.
This stone came from the field south of the Roman vallum, and
is just inside a wood to which the public has access. It is
now face down.
HOO781.   NZ 092 634.   PRUDHOE CASTLE.
Discovered built into the foundations of the 14th. Century
hall, this slab is on show.
HOO788.   NZ 0210 6480. THORNBOROUGH. (public path)
This displaced boulder lies under a fence on the public
footpath south of Thornborough High Barns.   There are wide
views south across the Tyne valley.
HOO782   NZ 982 648.   CORSTOPITUM. (E.H.)
The boulder was unearthed during excavation of the Roman site,
but no precise details were given. It is visible on site.
HOC783   NZ 909 703.   CHESTERS.(E.H.)
This used to be in the porch of the museum of the Roman site.
HOO766   NY 8293 7471 GOATSTONES (accessible).
This 'four poster', an arrangement of four small standing
stones, two with cupmarks, may have surrounded a burial.

Although there is now nothing to see of the stones on the
following three sites, they are recorded as simple cup-marked
stones that have appeared in later, Iron Age or Romano-British
settlements:
HOO764   NY 871 783 WEST FARM CAMP, BIRTLEY.
HOO765   NY 875 794 HIGH CARRY HOUSE, BIRTLEY.

HOO767   NY 9135 7485 GUNNER PEAK, BARRASFORD

HOO768   NY 9390 7460 SWINBURN STANDING STONE (Permission
needed). The largest standing stone in the county has cup
marks on its N. and S. faces. It stands in an intriguing
landscape of cultivation terraces and burial cairns.
HOO784 NY 9370 6559 ST.JOHN LEE STONE.(find spot, but stone in
the church). This finely- marked stone has chain marks that
suggest that it was dragged from the ridge to the field edge.
HOO784 NY 944 634 HEXHAM, SHIELD CROFT FARM,(a,b).
The stones were brought in with hardcore, so the original
location is unknown.

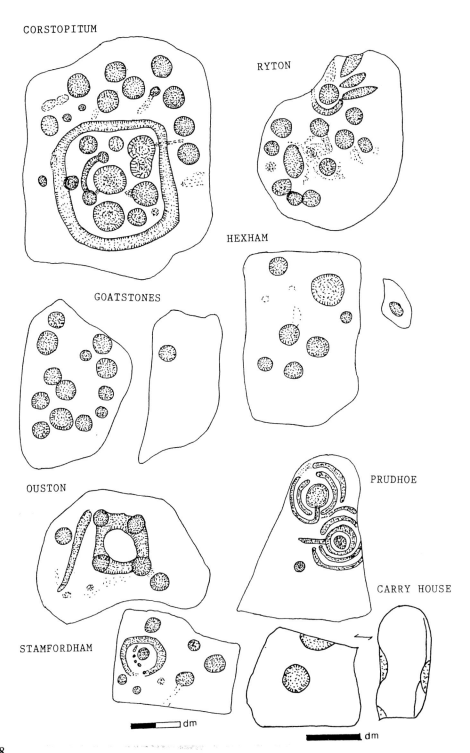

CORSTOPITUM

RYTON

HEXHAM

GOATSTONES

OUSTON

PRUDHOE

CARRY HOUSE

STAMFORDHAM

dm

dm

68

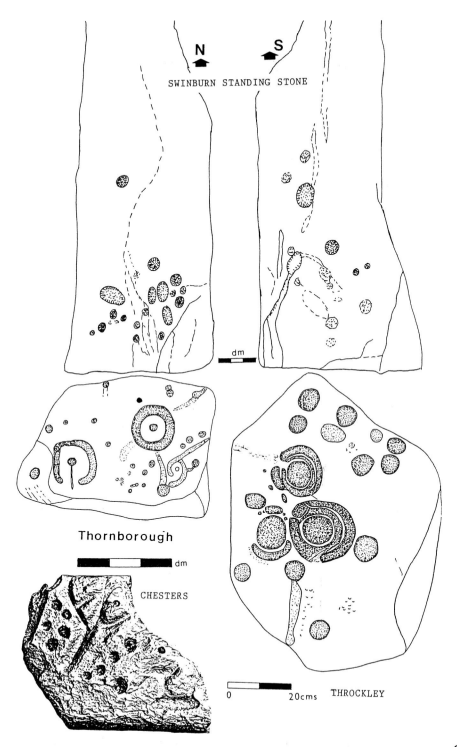

N   S

SWINBURN STANDING STONE

dm

Thornborough

dm

CHESTERS

0   20cms

THROCKLEY

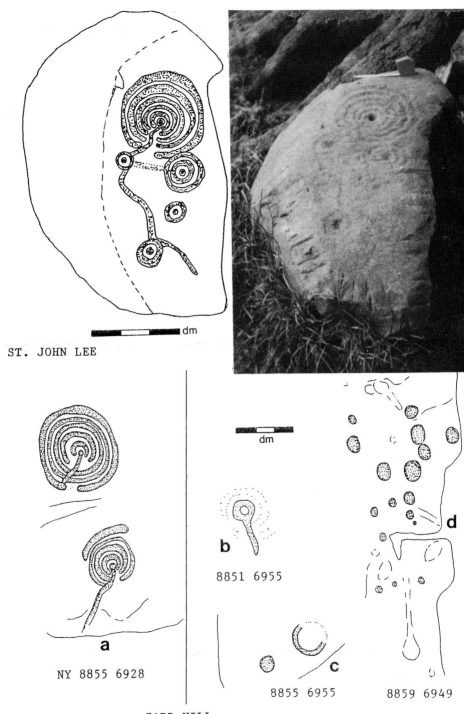

ST. JOHN LEE

dm

a

NY 8855 6928

b

8851 6955

c

8855 6955

d

8859 6949

dm

CARR HILL

HOO769 NY 886 693 CARR HILL, FRANKHAM FARM (private).
There are four stones in this group, two discovered by Jim Crow
and Ann Haigh. Although there are good views down the valley,
the site is not quite so open as others.
HOO810. NY 775 694. GREENLEE LOUGH (accessible)
The single cup-marked stone, flush with the surface, lies on
the edge of a Roman earth-walled 'camp' that proved to be
superimposed on earlier 'cord-rig' cultivation. To the NE. is
an abandoned settlement that has a curious marked rock which
may have been of prehistoric origin, but worked upon much
later.

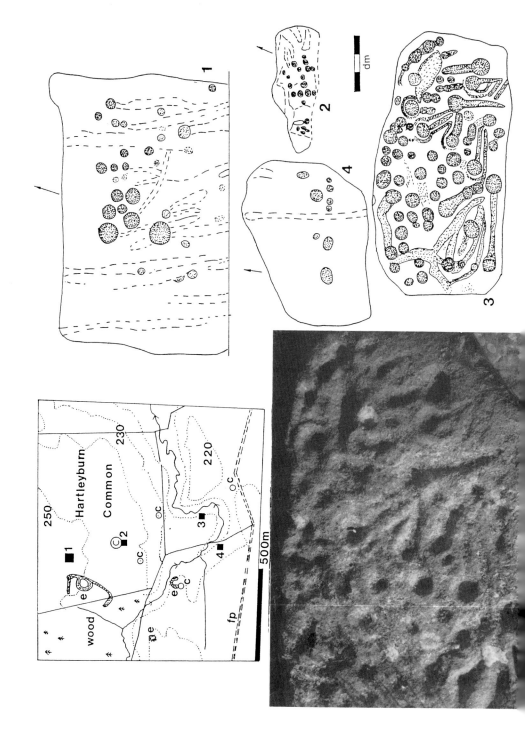

HOO770-3 HARTLEYBURN COMMON (some footpaths)
This big expanse of coarse grassland, coniferous woodland,
steep stream valleys and marsh, used for grazing, has
prehistoric enclosures that suggest a more ancient pastoral
role. Small round cairns seem to be burials rather than field
clearance.. There is quarried rock, but no cobblestones left.
The sandstone is naturally ridged, which gives an arrangement
of cups a more elaborate appearance. The four sites lie close
to the Cumbrian border.
1.HOO770   NY 6387 6131. On the edge of a quarry.
2.HOO771   NY 6395 6102. This kerbstone on a cairn has cups.
3.HOO772   NY 6412 6058. Now part of a ruined wall on a plateau
edge overlooking the Kellah Burn on the east. The natural
ridged surface has been used so that thin rings enter the
design. It seems to have been dragged to the field edge.
4.HOO773   NY 6395 6046. 9m. W. of the field wall from
Stanniston Hill to the Kellah Burn.

****

VOLUME 1
An amendment slip was included with most copies of Volume 1,
but the details are now entered here of Grid references for two
major sites:
CHATTON PARK HILL (page 51-56):
1. NU 0757 2906   2. NU 0757 2909   3. NU 0757 2909
4. NU 0723 2939   5. NU 0738 2941   6. NU 0742 2960
7. NU 0738 2941   8(a) portable, NU 0750 2938
8(b) portable, NU 0780 2930, now by the gate at the roadside.
9a NU 0775 2938   9b NU 0780 2933   10 NU 0773 2920
OLD BEWICK (page 51, 60-2):
The main rock in group 1 is a large, prominent block, with
others in the group widely scattered to the north,(a-h).
1a NU 0781 2158   2. NU 0076 2154.
Group 3 is among the scattered stone of a wall outside the hill
fort (a-g).   3a NU 0771 2160.
An old black and white photograph has come to light showing
that there is an important large mutiple-concentric motif with
a central cup and duct on a rock surface somewhere in the
ramparts of the double hillfort. It must be covered over, as
there is no trace of it.
UNPROVENANCED STONES
There are some stones in the store at the Museum of
Antiquities, Newcastle for which no locations are known.
Drawings of these are given below:.

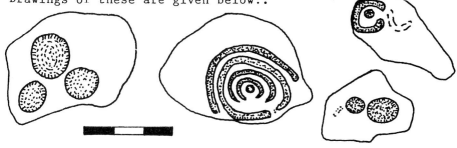

ADDED SITES
The most northerly stones in the County are found in a wall at
Berwick, between Longridge Towers and East Ord farm.
H00400 a-c NT 9645 5035(a,b), 9656 5040(c) East Ord.
The principal stone,(a), is in the north-facing wall. (b) is a
cup-marked portable, removed but safe. (c) is still at the
base of a destroyed part of the wall, and has a large cup. The
sketch is based on I.Hewitt's.
H00404 BROOMRIDGE 2 (page 8)
The drawing shows the complete motifs on the outcrop.
H00450 WEST HORTON 4 (page 22).
Listed previously, but not drawn, this small motif is on the
edge of a minor quarry near a diesel tank.
GUIDE POST, BEDLINGTON
Three well-made cups in metal-tooled stone are unlikely to be
prehistoric, but the drawing is included.
It is not always possible to be categorical about cupmarks; at
Rough Castles, Coe Crags, for example, a large detatched block
on the crag slope has marks that are a mixture of natural cups,
impact marks from bullets, and some possible man-made cups.

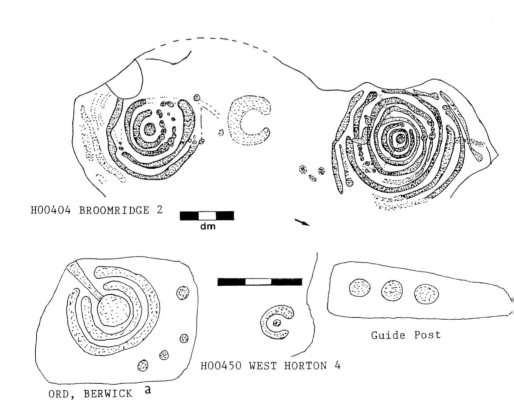

H00404 BROOMRIDGE 2
dm

ORD, BERWICK a

H00450 WEST HORTON 4

Guide Post

INDEX OF SITES

BIBLIOGRAPHY

The most comprehensive list of British sites, and detailed bibliography is in the <u>Proceedings of the Prehistoric Society,</u> <u>55, 1989.</u> pp. 45-88, by Ronald W.B.Morris.
A fully comprehensive bibliography for Northumberland is in preparation. Most of the references are in these publications:
1974 <u>The Prehistoric Carved Rocks of Northumberland</u> (Newcastle)
1983 <u>Northumberland's Prehistoric Rock Carvings.</u> (Rothbury)
This book contains a wide range of photographs of sites and details of pioneer discoveries. Although the new survey adds considerably to the corpus of rock art, this book is an essential part of it. It is in print, and available from Pendulum Publications, K.Bates, High Street, Rothbury, Morpeth.